LDAP: The Directory Protocol in Action

James Relington

DEDICATION

To those who seek knowledge, inspiration, and new perspectives—
may this book be a companion on your journey, a spark for curiosity,
and a reminder that every page turned is a step toward discovery.

AKNOWLEDGEMENTS

I would like to express my deepest gratitude to everyone who contributed to the creation of this book. To my colleagues and mentors, your insights and expertise have been invaluable. A special thank you to my family and friends for their unwavering support and encouragement throughout this journey.

Introduction to LDAP

The Lightweight Directory Access Protocol, commonly known as LDAP, is a cornerstone technology in the world of directory services and enterprise IT infrastructures. It serves as a protocol that allows users and applications to query and modify directory services over a network, making it a critical component in the management of identities, resources, and access controls across countless organizations. LDAP operates as an open, vendor-neutral, and standards-based protocol, designed to provide fast and efficient access to distributed directory information. Since its inception, LDAP has evolved into a highly scalable and versatile solution, powering some of the largest and most complex identity and access management ecosystems in the world.

At its core, LDAP is a protocol designed to facilitate access to information stored within a directory. Unlike traditional relational databases, which are optimized for transaction-heavy operations and complex relationships, directories are highly optimized for read-intensive operations with hierarchical data models. This fundamental difference is what allows LDAP to efficiently handle millions of queries per day in large environments, such as corporations, universities, and service providers. An LDAP directory typically stores information about users, groups, devices, services, and other resources that are essential to the operations of an organization. Commonly, this information is structured in a tree-like hierarchy, which mirrors real-world organizational structures, making it intuitive and practical for administrators and users alike.

The origins of LDAP can be traced back to the 1990s, when it was developed as a lightweight alternative to the heavyweight Directory Access Protocol used by X.500 directory services. X.500 was a comprehensive standard with complex requirements, including the use of the OSI networking stack, which limited its practical adoption. LDAP was designed to strip away much of the complexity of X.500, while retaining the essential capabilities needed to support modern directory services. By leveraging the simpler and widely used TCP/IP stack, LDAP quickly gained popularity and became the de facto standard for accessing directory services across various platforms.

LDAP is fundamentally a client-server protocol. Clients send requests to an LDAP server, which processes these requests and responds with the relevant information or confirmation of requested changes. The server, often referred to as a Directory System Agent (DSA), maintains the directory database and enforces the rules defined by its schema. The schema is a set of rules and definitions that dictate the structure of directory entries, including what attributes each type of entry may or must have. This structured and standardized approach ensures consistency and interoperability across different LDAP implementations and applications that interact with directory services.

An LDAP directory is organized into a hierarchy known as the Directory Information Tree, or DIT. This hierarchical structure resembles a tree with branches and leaves, where each node in the tree represents an entry. Each entry is uniquely identified by its

Distinguished Name (DN), which is a path-like representation of its location in the directory. For example, a user's entry might have a DN that reflects their position within a corporate structure, such as cn=John Doe,ou=Employees,dc=example,dc=com. This hierarchical naming convention allows administrators to easily locate and manage entries within the directory.

One of the key features of LDAP is its flexibility and extensibility. It can be used to store a wide variety of information beyond user credentials and access rights. Organizations often use LDAP directories to maintain information about organizational units, mailing lists, printers, servers, network devices, and even physical locations. The protocol supports a range of operations, including searching for entries, adding new entries, modifying existing entries, and deleting entries. In addition, LDAP supports complex filtering capabilities, enabling highly specific queries that can return precise results based on a wide range of criteria.

Security is a vital aspect of LDAP's role in enterprise environments. Given that LDAP directories often store sensitive information, including usernames, passwords, and access rights, securing communications between clients and servers is essential. LDAP supports several methods of securing these communications, including the use of SSL/TLS to encrypt data in transit and Simple Authentication and Security Layer (SASL) mechanisms for more advanced authentication scenarios. Access control lists (ACLs) are also a common feature in LDAP implementations, providing administrators with the ability to finely control which users and applications can access or modify specific parts of the directory.

Over time, LDAP has become a critical component in identity management and authentication systems. It is frequently integrated with other technologies such as Kerberos, RADIUS, and SAML to provide comprehensive authentication, authorization, and accounting (AAA) solutions. LDAP directories often serve as the authoritative source of identity information for Single Sign-On (SSO) systems, enabling users to authenticate once and gain access to multiple services without repeated login prompts. This centralized approach to identity and access management simplifies administration, enhances security, and improves the user experience.

Today, LDAP remains highly relevant despite the emergence of newer technologies and protocols. Its resilience and adaptability have allowed it to persist in modern IT landscapes, where it continues to serve as the backbone for countless authentication and directory services worldwide. Whether integrated with legacy systems or deployed as part of cutting-edge cloud-native architectures, LDAP's role as a reliable, efficient, and scalable directory access protocol is as significant as ever. As organizations continue to navigate the evolving challenges of identity management and cybersecurity, LDAP stands as a trusted and proven technology at the heart of many critical systems.

The History of Directory Services

The history of directory services is closely tied to the evolution of computer networks and enterprise computing. As organizations began to grow their IT infrastructures in the late twentieth century, the need for centralized management of users, devices, and resources became increasingly critical. Early computing environments relied heavily on isolated systems, where user accounts and configuration data were stored locally on individual machines. This approach worked adequately in small or standalone environments but quickly became impractical as networks expanded and organizations began connecting hundreds or thousands of computers together. The concept of a centralized directory service emerged as a solution to the growing need for a unified repository of information that could be accessed across multiple systems and applications.

The origins of directory services can be traced back to the 1980s, during the development of networked computing and the advent of the Open Systems Interconnection (OSI) model. One of the earliest and most influential directory service standards was the X.500 series, developed by the International Telecommunication Union (ITU) and the International Organization for Standardization (ISO). X.500 was designed as part of the OSI suite of protocols and aimed to provide a comprehensive framework for managing directory information in distributed environments. The X.500 model introduced several concepts that would become foundational in directory services, such as the Directory Information Tree (DIT), Distinguished Names (DNs), and a strict schema structure to define directory entries and attributes.

X.500 was a groundbreaking achievement in terms of directory service design, but it was also complex and resource-intensive. Its reliance on the OSI networking stack made it challenging to implement and limited its adoption in many organizations. The complexity of the protocol and its heavyweight nature meant that it did not gain widespread traction outside of certain specialized industries and government sectors. Nevertheless, X.500 laid the groundwork for what would become more streamlined and accessible directory service technologies in the years to follow.

As TCP/IP gained dominance as the networking standard of the internet and enterprise environments in the late 1980s and early 1990s, it became clear that a lighter and more efficient alternative to X.500 was needed. This led to the development of the Lightweight Directory Access Protocol, or LDAP. LDAP was designed as a simplified version of X.500, retaining many of its core concepts while operating over the more common and easier-to-implement TCP/IP protocol suite. LDAP reduced the complexity of directory access, provided faster performance, and lowered the barrier to entry for organizations looking to deploy directory services.

LDAP was originally developed at the University of Michigan in the early 1990s as part of a project to create a more efficient means of accessing X.500 directories. However, it soon evolved beyond its initial role as a mere gateway to X.500 systems. As LDAP matured, it became a fully standalone directory access protocol, capable of interfacing with lightweight directory services that did not rely on the full X.500 infrastructure. This shift marked a turning point in the history of directory services, as LDAP rapidly gained adoption in both academic and commercial sectors.

By the mid-1990s, the increasing popularity of LDAP led to the development of several commercial and open-source directory servers that implemented the protocol natively. Notable examples include the Netscape Directory Server, the Microsoft Active Directory, the OpenLDAP project, and Novell eDirectory. These directory servers provided organizations with robust, scalable, and interoperable solutions for managing user accounts, devices, and other network resources. LDAP's adoption was further fueled by its integration into emerging identity management and authentication systems, where it became a critical component for managing user credentials and controlling access to networked services.

During the same period, directory services began playing a crucial role in supporting authentication protocols and access control mechanisms. Kerberos, an authentication protocol developed at the Massachusetts Institute of Technology (MIT), leveraged directory services to store and retrieve key authentication data. Similarly, the rise of Single Sign-On (SSO) solutions and centralized authentication frameworks highlighted the need for reliable directory services that could act as authoritative sources of identity information.

The late 1990s and early 2000s saw directory services become even more integral to enterprise IT environments as businesses began adopting Microsoft's Active Directory in large numbers. Introduced with Windows 2000 Server, Active Directory combined LDAP, Kerberos, and DNS technologies into a unified and highly integrated directory service platform. Its deep integration with the Windows operating system and enterprise applications made Active Directory a dominant force in corporate IT, with millions of organizations worldwide relying on it to manage users, computers, and security policies.

At the same time, the open-source movement gained momentum, and projects such as OpenLDAP provided an alternative to proprietary directory services. OpenLDAP enabled organizations to deploy cost-effective and customizable directory solutions that adhered to open standards. This period also saw the expansion of LDAP's role beyond traditional IT environments, as web-based applications, email systems, and enterprise resource planning (ERP) platforms began integrating with LDAP directories for authentication and user data management.

In more recent years, the shift towards cloud computing, hybrid environments, and identity-as-a-service (IDaaS) offerings has further transformed the landscape of directory services. While traditional on-premises directory services like Active Directory and OpenLDAP continue to be widely used, new cloud-native directory platforms have emerged to address the needs of modern organizations. Services such as Azure Active Directory, Okta Universal Directory, and AWS Directory Service provide scalable, cloud-based identity management solutions that integrate with a wide array of applications and services.

Despite the introduction of these newer platforms, the foundational principles established by early directory service protocols like X.500 and LDAP remain highly relevant. The hierarchical structure of directory data, the use of schemas to enforce data consistency, and the reliance on standardized access protocols continue to be core components of modern directory services. The history of directory services is one of continual adaptation and innovation, driven by the changing needs of organizations and advancements in technology. From the early days of X.500 to the widespread adoption of LDAP and the rise of cloud-based directories, directory services have evolved into a critical pillar of enterprise computing and identity management.

LDAP Architecture Overview

The architecture of LDAP is built on a simple yet highly effective client-server model that enables efficient and secure access to directory information over a network. At its core, LDAP is designed to provide fast query performance and easy retrieval of hierarchical data. This makes LDAP an essential part of enterprise environments, where organizations require a scalable, centralized solution for managing identity-related information. The basic components of LDAP architecture include LDAP clients, LDAP servers, and the directory information itself, which is organized and accessed through a well-defined protocol.

LDAP clients are applications or tools that send requests to an LDAP server. These clients can range from command-line utilities used by system administrators to full-scale applications integrated into enterprise systems. The role of the client is to initiate operations such as search, add, modify, or delete entries in the directory. LDAP clients rely on a standard set of operations defined by the protocol to communicate with the server. The communication typically occurs over TCP/IP, which allows LDAP to operate in a wide variety of network environments, from local area networks to global enterprise networks.

At the other end of the communication is the LDAP server, also known as the Directory System Agent (DSA). The server is responsible for processing requests from LDAP clients and managing the directory database. The server stores directory entries in a structured and hierarchical format that reflects the organization of the directory information tree, or DIT. The DIT is the backbone of the LDAP directory, where each entry is placed within a tree-like hierarchy. This hierarchical organization is based on domain components, organizational units, and common names, which together form a Distinguished Name (DN) for each entry. The DN acts as a unique identifier for directory entries, making it possible for clients to target specific objects within the directory.

Each directory entry within the DIT is composed of a set of attributes and an object class. Attributes are name-value pairs that describe the characteristics of the entry. For example, a user entry might include attributes such as uid for the user ID, cn for the common name, mail for the email address, and userPassword for the password hash. The object class defines the structural role of the entry and dictates which attributes are required and which are optional. Object classes are part of the directory schema, which serves as the blueprint for all directory entries. The schema enforces consistency and ensures that directory data adheres to a predefined format, which is essential for interoperability across different systems and applications.

LDAP architecture also includes a variety of operations that clients can perform on directory entries. The most common operation is the search, where clients query the directory to locate entries that match specific criteria. Search operations can be fine-tuned using filters, allowing clients to retrieve only the entries that meet certain conditions. For example, a search filter might be designed to return all users in a particular organizational unit or all entries with a specific attribute value. Other important operations include bind, which establishes an authenticated session between the client and server; add, which creates new entries in the directory; modify, which updates existing entries; delete, which removes entries; and unbind, which terminates the session.

An essential feature of LDAP architecture is its ability to support secure and controlled access to directory information. LDAP servers can enforce access control policies using Access Control Lists (ACLs). These lists define which users or systems are allowed to perform specific operations on directory entries or attributes. For example, a directory administrator might configure ACLs to allow regular users to read their own account information but restrict them from modifying critical attributes or accessing sensitive data belonging to other users. This fine-grained access control mechanism ensures that only authorized entities can interact with the directory in specific ways, which is vital for maintaining data security and integrity.

To further enhance security, LDAP supports multiple authentication methods. The simplest method is anonymous access, where no authentication is performed, but this is rarely used in production environments. More commonly, clients authenticate using simple bind, where a DN and password are sent to the server, or through more advanced methods such as Simple Authentication and Security Layer (SASL) mechanisms, which allow for integration with external authentication systems like Kerberos. Additionally, LDAP supports encryption using SSL/TLS, which ensures that data exchanged between clients and servers is protected from eavesdropping and tampering during transit.

Another important aspect of LDAP architecture is its support for replication. In large-scale environments, a single LDAP server may not be sufficient to handle all client requests or provide the required availability and fault tolerance. LDAP replication allows directory data to be copied and synchronized across multiple servers, creating a distributed directory service that can operate reliably even in the face of hardware failures or network outages. Replication can be configured in different ways, including single-master replication, where one server acts as the authoritative source for updates, and multi-master replication, where updates can occur on any server and are synchronized across the system. This capability ensures that directory services can scale effectively to meet the demands of modern enterprises.

LDAP servers also often include additional components such as referral and chaining mechanisms. Referrals allow an LDAP server to direct a client to another server when a requested entry is outside its own directory tree. Chaining occurs when a server forwards a client's request to another server and then returns the result as if it came from the original server. These mechanisms enable LDAP directories to be federated across multiple domains or organizations, supporting complex, distributed directory topologies.

The efficiency and flexibility of LDAP architecture have made it a key technology for a wide range of applications, from identity management and access control to address book services and network resource discovery. Its modular and standards-based design allows LDAP to integrate with numerous systems and technologies, making it a foundational element of enterprise IT infrastructure. By providing a reliable and scalable way to store, organize, and access directory information, LDAP architecture continues to play a critical role in supporting the operational needs of organizations worldwide.

LDAP vs. Other Directory Protocols

LDAP has long been regarded as one of the most prominent directory access protocols, but it exists within a broader ecosystem of directory protocols that have evolved over time to address different needs. Comparing LDAP to other directory protocols helps to understand its unique characteristics, strengths, and limitations in various contexts. While LDAP has become the de facto standard for directory access, other protocols such as X.500's Directory Access Protocol (DAP), Microsoft's proprietary protocols integrated into Active Directory, and more modern approaches like SCIM (System for Cross-domain Identity Management) offer alternative methods for interacting with directory services.

The most direct comparison is between LDAP and its predecessor, DAP, which was introduced as part of the X.500 directory standard in the late 1980s. DAP was developed to provide a comprehensive and highly structured means of accessing directory information, operating within the OSI networking model. It offered a rich set of features and capabilities but came with significant complexity and overhead. The OSI stack required for DAP's operation was cumbersome, resource-intensive, and difficult to integrate with the increasingly popular TCP/IP-based networks of the time. This complexity limited DAP's widespread adoption outside of certain niche environments, such as government and military systems. LDAP emerged as a lightweight alternative to DAP, simplifying the protocol by eliminating dependencies on the OSI model and allowing directory access over TCP/IP. By retaining many of the logical structures of X.500 while reducing the networking and implementation complexity, LDAP provided a more practical and accessible solution for most organizations. LDAP's streamlined approach, combined with its performance improvements and interoperability, allowed it to surpass DAP and become the preferred directory protocol in commercial and open-source systems.

Another significant point of comparison is between LDAP and the proprietary protocols that Microsoft integrated into its Active Directory environment. While Active Directory is built on LDAP for directory access, it also incorporates several additional protocols and services to create a tightly integrated identity and access management solution. For example, Active Directory uses Kerberos for authentication, which allows for secure, ticket-based logins across Windows domains. It also relies on the Global Catalog protocol to facilitate searches across multiple domains and forest structures within large enterprise environments. While LDAP provides a standard method for querying and modifying directory entries, Microsoft's extensions in Active Directory include Group Policy Objects (GPOs), which allow administrators to enforce policies on users and computers within the domain. These additional layers of functionality give Active Directory capabilities that go beyond the traditional LDAP model. However, the proprietary nature of Active Directory and its deeper integration with Microsoft's ecosystem can create challenges when organizations attempt to integrate it with non-Microsoft platforms. LDAP, in contrast, maintains its status as a vendor-neutral protocol and is supported across a wide range of operating systems and applications.

As directory and identity management requirements have evolved, so too have alternative protocols that address newer challenges. One of the notable examples is SCIM, a modern protocol designed specifically for cloud-based environments and identity management across domains. SCIM emerged as organizations began to shift towards cloud services and required more efficient ways to automate user provisioning and deprovisioning across multiple platforms. Unlike LDAP, which focuses primarily on directory access and queries within hierarchical directory trees, SCIM is optimized for RESTful APIs and JSON-based data exchange, making it well-suited for modern web services and microservices architectures. SCIM provides a standardized approach for synchronizing identity data across SaaS platforms, cloud directories, and other identity providers. It is lightweight, easy to integrate with web applications, and reduces the complexity associated with traditional LDAP deployments. However, SCIM does not attempt to replace LDAP's core function as a directory access protocol within traditional enterprise environments. Instead, it complements LDAP by addressing gaps in automation and interoperability across distributed cloud services.

Another noteworthy protocol is RADIUS (Remote Authentication Dial-In User Service), which, while not a directory protocol in the conventional sense, often works alongside directory services to provide authentication, authorization, and accounting functionality, particularly for network access control. RADIUS operates using a client-server model similar to LDAP but is optimized for scenarios where authentication requests are sent by network devices such as VPN concentrators, wireless access points, and network switches. RADIUS typically leverages an LDAP directory or other user database on the backend to validate credentials, making it an essential component in enterprise networking environments. However, RADIUS is limited in its directory access capabilities compared to LDAP. It is primarily concerned with authentication workflows and lacks LDAP's robust querying and modification features for managing directory entries.

The comparison between LDAP and newer identity federation protocols such as SAML (Security Assertion Markup Language) and OpenID Connect (OIDC) highlights the divergence between traditional directory access and federated identity management. While LDAP focuses on storing and retrieving structured identity data within a centralized directory, SAML and OIDC are designed to facilitate single sign-on (SSO) and identity federation across organizational boundaries. These protocols enable users to authenticate with one service and gain access to multiple independent systems using secure tokens or assertions. LDAP directories often serve as authoritative identity stores for SSO solutions that rely on SAML or OIDC. However, LDAP itself is not a protocol for federated identity; rather, it provides the user data required by identity providers and service providers participating in federated authentication workflows.

Despite the availability of alternative protocols and solutions, LDAP remains a critical piece of enterprise infrastructure due to its maturity, wide support, and ability to manage structured, hierarchical identity data efficiently. Its flexibility allows it to integrate with various technologies, including those mentioned above, creating hybrid environments where LDAP directories work alongside SSO solutions, RADIUS servers, and SCIM-based cloud identity platforms. Organizations continue to rely on LDAP as the backbone for internal directory services, while layering additional protocols and technologies to address specific use cases related to security, automation, and cloud adoption.

The longevity and continued relevance of LDAP can be attributed to its adherence to open standards, broad interoperability, and proven track record in managing directory services at scale. While other protocols may offer specialized capabilities or better fit modern cloud-centric architectures, LDAP's robust querying capabilities, extensible schema design, and ability to operate in distributed environments ensure its role as a foundational technology in identity and access management. Understanding the differences between LDAP and these other protocols allows organizations to make informed decisions about how to architect their identity services in alignment with their operational and security requirements.

The LDAP Information Model

The LDAP information model is the fundamental framework that defines how data is represented, structured, and managed within an LDAP directory. It is a critical part of how LDAP organizes and processes information, providing the rules and concepts that govern the storage and retrieval of directory entries. The model is hierarchical and object-oriented, supporting a flexible yet rigidly defined way of handling identity-related data. Understanding the LDAP information model is key to deploying and managing directory services effectively, as it impacts how administrators structure their directory tree, create entries, and enforce consistency across the entire system.

At the core of the LDAP information model is the concept of entries. An entry is a collection of related information about an object, such as a person, device, service, or organizational unit. Each entry in the directory is uniquely identified by its Distinguished Name, or DN, which specifies its exact location within the Directory Information Tree. The DN is composed of a sequence of Relative Distinguished Names, or RDNs, which describe the entry's position relative to its parent within the hierarchy. For example, an entry representing a user in the accounting department of a company might have a DN like cn=Jane Smith,ou=Accounting,dc=example,dc=com. This hierarchical structure mirrors the organization's internal structure, making it intuitive to navigate and manage.

Each entry is made up of a set of attributes, which are name-value pairs that define the characteristics of the entry. Attributes can hold a variety of data, including strings, numbers, and binary data. Common attribute types include cn for common name, sn for surname, uid for user identifier, mail for email address, and objectClass to define the type of object. Attributes may be single-valued, meaning they can hold only one value, or multi-valued, allowing multiple values for the same attribute. For instance, a user entry might have multiple values for the mail attribute to represent several email addresses. The flexibility of attribute design enables administrators to capture a wide range of information within directory entries while maintaining a consistent structure.

Object classes are another essential component of the LDAP information model. An object class defines the schema rules that apply to an entry. These rules specify what attributes an entry must have, what attributes are optional, and how the entry fits into the directory hierarchy. Object classes are organized into three categories: structural, auxiliary, and abstract. Structural object classes define the primary type of an entry and must be present for every entry in the directory. For example, the person or organizationalUnit object classes are commonly used structural classes. Auxiliary object classes provide additional attributes that can be added to entries that already belong to a structural object class. For instance, the posixAccount auxiliary class can be applied to user entries to add attributes required by UNIX systems. Abstract object classes are rarely used directly and serve primarily as templates for creating structural classes.

The schema in LDAP is the repository of all object classes, attribute types, matching rules, and syntaxes used within the directory. It defines the vocabulary and constraints of the directory, ensuring that entries adhere to a consistent and predictable structure. The schema is extensible, meaning administrators can add custom object classes and attributes to meet the specific needs of their organization. However, extending the schema requires careful planning to avoid conflicts and ensure compatibility with applications that depend on the directory. Many LDAP servers come with a default schema that includes commonly used object classes such as inetOrgPerson, organizationalUnit, and groupOfNames, which are suitable for most standard deployments.

One of the distinguishing characteristics of the LDAP information model is its hierarchical organization of data through the Directory Information Tree. The DIT represents all the entries in the directory as a tree structure, starting from a single root entry and branching out into progressively more specific entries. The root entry, sometimes called the root DSE (DSA-specific entry), often represents the organization's domain, such as dc=example,dc=com. Below the root, branches might represent organizational units, departments, or geographic locations. The hierarchical nature of the DIT supports delegation of administrative responsibilities and provides a clear and logical framework for navigating the directory. For example, an administrator might delegate control of the ou=Sales subtree to a regional manager, who can then manage user accounts and resources within that specific organizational unit.

The LDAP information model also defines the concept of referrals and aliases. A referral allows an LDAP server to direct a client to another server if the requested entry does not exist within its own DIT. This enables distributed directory architectures where data is spread across multiple servers. An alias is a pointer to another entry within the directory, functioning similarly to a symbolic link in a file system. Aliases help reduce data duplication and simplify directory maintenance by allowing one entry to serve multiple purposes within the tree structure.

Matching rules are another integral part of the LDAP information model. These rules define how attribute values are compared during search operations. For example, a caseIgnoreMatch rule might be used for the cn attribute to ensure that searches are case-insensitive. Matching rules are closely tied to attribute syntaxes, which define the data types allowed for attributes, such as directory strings, integers, or distinguished names. Together, syntaxes and matching rules determine how data is validated and queried, influencing both directory performance and accuracy in search results.

In the context of directory searches, the LDAP information model supports powerful filtering capabilities. Filters use logical operators such as AND, OR, and NOT, along with comparison operators like equality, presence, and substring matching, to narrow down search results. These filtering mechanisms allow clients to retrieve highly specific information from large directories efficiently. For instance, a filter could be designed to return all users in a particular department who have a specific job title and an active status attribute.

The information model also plays a significant role in LDAP replication and synchronization processes. Since the directory structure and schema are standardized across all participating servers, replication mechanisms can reliably synchronize directory entries, ensuring data consistency and availability across distributed systems. The structured and predictable nature of the LDAP information model enables efficient data synchronization, minimizing conflicts and ensuring that directory clients always receive up-to-date information.

Overall, the LDAP information model provides a rigorous yet adaptable framework for representing directory data. It balances flexibility with structure, offering administrators and developers the tools to design scalable, secure, and consistent directory services. By enforcing clear rules for entry composition, hierarchical organization, and data validation, the information model is a key factor behind

LDAP's long-standing success and widespread adoption in enterprise environments.

Understanding LDAP Schemas

The LDAP schema is a crucial component of any directory service, acting as the blueprint that defines how data is structured, validated, and organized within the directory. Without the schema, the directory would lack the rules and constraints necessary to ensure data consistency and interoperability across clients and servers. The schema governs which object classes and attributes can be used in directory entries, how these attributes are formatted, and how they relate to one another. It is this well-defined structure that enables LDAP directories to function efficiently as repositories for identity information, resources, and configuration data.

At its most basic level, an LDAP schema is composed of object classes, attribute types, matching rules, and syntaxes. Each of these elements plays a distinct role in shaping the directory's data model. Object classes serve as templates that define the types of entries that can exist within the directory. They specify which attributes an entry must include and which attributes are optional. For example, the widely used inetOrgPerson object class is often applied to user entries and requires attributes such as cn (common name) and sn (surname), while allowing optional attributes like telephoneNumber, mail, and employeeNumber. The rigid structure enforced by object classes ensures that all entries of a certain type share a common set of attributes, making data management and queries more predictable and reliable.

Attribute types, on the other hand, define the individual pieces of information that make up an entry. Each attribute type has a name, an object identifier (OID), and is associated with a specific syntax that dictates the format of its values. For instance, the mail attribute is used to store email addresses and follows the directory string syntax, which allows for text-based input. Attribute types can also specify whether they are single-valued, meaning they accept only one value, or multi-valued, allowing them to hold multiple values. This is important when modeling real-world scenarios, such as a user who has multiple email addresses or a group that has multiple member entries.

In addition to object classes and attribute types, the LDAP schema includes matching rules, which define how attribute values are compared during search operations and data validation. Matching rules are essential for directory queries, as they determine whether two attribute values are considered equivalent. For example, a caseIgnoreMatch rule might be applied to the cn attribute to ensure that searches are case-insensitive, so that cn=John Doe and cn=john doe would be treated as matching values. Different matching rules are available for different attribute syntaxes, allowing for fine-tuned search behaviors depending on the data type. Common matching rules include equalityMatch for exact matches, substringMatch for partial matches, and orderingMatch for attributes that support sorted queries.

The syntax associated with each attribute type defines the acceptable format for its values. Syntaxes ensure that data is stored and interpreted consistently across the directory. LDAP provides a variety of syntaxes, including directory string, which supports UTF-8 encoded text; integer, for numerical values; boolean, for true/false values; and distinguished name, for references to other entries in the directory. Syntax enforcement plays a critical role in data integrity, as it prevents invalid or incompatible data from being added to the directory. For example, an attribute with integer syntax will reject any non-numeric values during entry creation or modification.

LDAP schemas are designed to be extensible, meaning organizations can define custom object classes and attribute types to meet their specific needs. This flexibility is particularly valuable for enterprises that require specialized data to be stored alongside standard directory information. Custom schema elements are typically defined in an LDIF (LDAP Data Interchange Format) file and then imported into the directory server. When creating custom schema components, administrators must assign unique OIDs to prevent conflicts with existing schema elements and ensure that custom attributes and object classes follow established naming conventions. Careful schema design is important because poorly planned extensions can lead to inconsistencies, reduced interoperability with other applications, and complications during directory upgrades or migrations.

The default schema provided by most LDAP servers includes a comprehensive set of object classes and attributes suitable for common use cases. For example, the core schema defines basic structural object classes like organization, organizationalUnit, and person. Additionally, the cosine and inetOrgPerson schemas extend the core functionality to support more complex organizational and user data models. Many servers also include schemas tailored for integration with specific technologies, such as the nis schema for UNIX system compatibility or the samba schema for integration with Samba-based file sharing services. These pre-defined schemas offer a solid foundation for directory deployments, but administrators must often tailor them to fit the unique requirements of their environment.

Schema management is a critical responsibility for directory administrators. Any changes to the schema, such as adding new object classes or modifying existing ones, must be carefully tested in development environments before being applied to production systems. Inconsistent or improperly designed schema changes can cause serious issues, including data corruption, application failures, and interoperability problems. Many modern LDAP servers support dynamic schema updates, allowing changes to be made without restarting the server. However, this convenience does not eliminate the need for thorough planning and validation, especially in large or distributed directory environments where multiple applications and services rely on consistent schema definitions.

Schema design also plays a significant role in performance optimization. The selection of attribute types, the use of indexing, and the enforcement of attribute constraints all influence how efficiently the directory processes queries and updates. For example, frequently queried attributes, such as uid or mail, are often indexed to speed up search operations. Without proper indexing, the directory server might perform full-tree scans during queries, resulting in slow response times. Likewise, enforcing strict attribute syntaxes and minimizing the use of multi-valued attributes where unnecessary can reduce storage overhead and improve data retrieval efficiency.

In distributed directory environments, schema consistency is vital for replication and synchronization processes. When multiple LDAP servers are involved in a replication topology, all participating servers must share an identical schema to avoid replication errors and data mismatches. This requirement adds another layer of complexity to schema management, particularly in multi-master replication scenarios where changes can originate from any server. Directory administrators must ensure that schema changes are propagated uniformly across all servers and validated before replication takes place.

Understanding LDAP schemas is essential for building robust and scalable directory services. The schema defines the rules of engagement for how data is structured, stored, and accessed within the directory, providing a foundation for effective identity and resource management. Whether using default schemas or designing custom extensions, administrators must approach schema development with a strategic mindset, balancing flexibility with consistency and ensuring that the directory remains efficient, interoperable, and secure.

LDAP Naming Model and DIT

The LDAP naming model and Directory Information Tree, or DIT, form the backbone of how information is organized and referenced within an LDAP directory. The naming model defines how entries are uniquely identified, while the DIT describes the hierarchical structure in which those entries exist. Together, they provide a logical and navigable framework for administrators and clients to locate, manage, and manipulate directory information efficiently. The LDAP directory is not a flat database but a structured tree where every object has a distinct place within a well-defined hierarchy. Understanding how the naming model and DIT function is crucial for designing and operating LDAP-based systems in any organization.

In LDAP, every entry is assigned a Distinguished Name, or DN. The DN is the unique identifier for an entry and specifies its position in the DIT. Unlike a database table where rows are typically identified by numeric IDs or keys, LDAP uses the DN to represent the full path to an entry from the root of the directory. The DN is made up of one or more Relative Distinguished Names, or RDNs, which identify the entry relative to its immediate parent in the tree. The RDN is typically based on a single attribute, such as cn for common name or ou for organizational unit. For instance, the RDN for a user named Alice might be cn=Alice, while the RDN for the finance department might be ou=Finance. The combination of these RDNs creates a hierarchical path that results in a DN like cn=Alice,ou=Finance,dc=example,dc=com.

The hierarchical structure of the DIT is modeled after a tree, starting from a root node and branching out into organizational units, domains, and individual entries. The root of the tree is often defined by domain components, or dc elements, which reflect the organization's internet domain. For example, an organization with the domain example.com might have a root DN of dc=example,dc=com. From there, branches are created to represent departments, geographical locations, or other logical groupings, resulting in a structure that mirrors the organization's real-world layout. This design allows administrators to create an intuitive directory hierarchy where users, groups, devices, and services are organized logically.

The use of hierarchical naming provides several practical advantages. First, it simplifies administration by grouping related entries together under common parent nodes. For example, placing all user accounts for the Sales department under ou=Sales makes it easy to apply policies, permissions, or searches that target that specific organizational unit. Second, it supports delegated administration, where different teams or departments can manage their own branches of the tree without interfering with others. Third, the hierarchical nature of the DIT makes LDAP queries more efficient, as searches can be scoped to specific subtrees to limit the scope of the search operation and reduce server load.

Each entry in the DIT must have a unique DN, but entries may share the same RDN if they reside in different branches. For example, it is entirely possible to have cn=John Smith,ou=Engineering,dc=example,dc=com and cn=John Smith,ou=HR,dc=example,dc=com coexist within the same directory because their DNs are unique despite having identical RDNs. This characteristic allows organizations to reuse naming conventions across different departments or regions without causing conflicts.

The DIT not only organizes user accounts but also accommodates other types of entries. Organizational units, groups, roles, devices, printers, servers, and other resources can all be represented within the tree. Object classes such as organizationalUnit, groupOfNames, and device are used to define the structure and attributes of these entries. The flexibility of the LDAP naming model allows organizations to design a directory structure that fits their specific operational needs, whether that means grouping users by location, department, or job function, or combining multiple criteria to create a multi-level hierarchy.

LDAP supports several naming conventions, but one of the most widely used is the domain component-based model, where the top of the tree corresponds to the organization's internet domain. This approach has become standard practice because it aligns with DNS naming, providing consistency between the directory and other network services. In some cases, organizations might adopt alternative naming strategies based on X.500 recommendations, using country codes (c), locality names (l), and organization names (o) as the top-level structure. However, domain components (dc) have generally become the preferred convention due to their simplicity and compatibility with internet-centric architectures.

Another important aspect of the LDAP naming model is its support for aliases and referrals. Aliases are entries that point to other entries within the directory, effectively creating shortcuts within the DIT. This can be useful in scenarios where an entry needs to appear in multiple locations without duplicating data. Referrals, on the other hand, allow an LDAP server to direct a client to another server if the requested data resides outside its own DIT. This is particularly valuable in distributed directory environments where multiple LDAP servers manage different portions of the overall directory. Referrals enable the creation of a federated directory system where clients can seamlessly navigate between servers based on the DNs they query.

The naming model also defines how LDAP operations, such as search, add, modify, and delete, interact with directory entries. When performing a search, the client specifies a base DN, which acts as the starting point of the search within the tree. The search scope can be limited to the base object itself, to a single level below the base DN, or to the entire subtree starting from the base DN. This scoping mechanism is one of the key features of LDAP that leverages the hierarchical nature of the DIT to optimize performance and precision in directory queries.

The logical structure provided by the LDAP naming model is closely tied to real-world organizational practices. Many enterprises design their DIT to reflect corporate hierarchies, with branches for each department or regional office. Others might organize the DIT around functional roles, job titles, or access control boundaries. The choice of structure depends on how the organization intends to manage users and resources. The flexibility of LDAP allows for a variety of design patterns, but careful planning is essential to avoid creating a disorganized or inefficient DIT. A poorly designed tree can lead to administrative overhead, performance issues, and difficulties in applying consistent access controls.

LDAP also supports schema constraints that affect naming. For example, certain object classes specify mandatory attributes that are often used in RDNs. The organizationalUnit object class requires an ou attribute, which is commonly used as an RDN for departments or units. The person or inetOrgPerson object classes usually employ cn or uid as part of the entry's RDN. The combination of object class rules and directory schema helps enforce consistency in how entries are named and organized.

The LDAP naming model and DIT are foundational to directory services because they determine how every interaction with the directory is framed. Whether adding a new user, modifying a device entry, or running a search query, the DN and its relationship within the tree dictate how the operation is performed and how data is retrieved or updated. By mastering the concepts of the naming model and the DIT, administrators can design LDAP directories that are both scalable and easy to manage, ensuring that the directory service remains a reliable and efficient component of the organization's IT infrastructure.

Distinguished Names and Relative Distinguished Names

In the LDAP directory model, the concepts of Distinguished Names (DNs) and Relative Distinguished Names (RDNs) are central to how data is organized, identified, and accessed. These naming mechanisms are foundational to LDAP's hierarchical structure, providing the means by which entries within the Directory Information Tree, or DIT, are uniquely referenced and located. The relationship between DNs and RDNs forms the basis for navigation and data manipulation in LDAP, and understanding these elements is critical for anyone involved in directory service design, administration, or integration.

A Distinguished Name is the unique identifier for an entry in the LDAP directory. It defines the exact location of the entry within the DIT, much like a full file path defines the location of a file within a file system. Every entry in the directory, from a user account to a printer object, has a DN that sets it apart from all other entries. The DN is composed of one or more Relative Distinguished Names, which are concatenated in a sequence to describe the path from the entry back to the root of the tree. Each RDN corresponds to a level within the directory hierarchy and contains one or more attribute-value pairs that uniquely identify the entry relative to its parent node.

For example, consider the DN cn=John Smith,ou=Engineering,dc=example,dc=com. In this DN, cn=John Smith is the RDN identifying the user entry under the Engineering organizational unit, ou=Engineering is the RDN for the Engineering department under the base domain, and dc=example,dc=com represents the domain components at the root level of the tree. When read from left to right, this DN defines a clear hierarchical path, starting from the leaf entry representing John Smith and moving upwards through the parent containers until reaching the domain root.

Relative Distinguished Names, by definition, are the naming elements that distinguish an entry from its siblings at the same level within the directory tree. An RDN is usually composed of a single attribute-value pair, but it can also include multiple pairs if needed to ensure uniqueness. For example, an entry might use cn=John

Smith+employeeNumber=1234 as its RDN, combining both the common name and a unique employee number to differentiate it from other entries that may share the same common name within the same organizational unit. While single-attribute RDNs are more common due to their simplicity, multi-attribute RDNs offer additional flexibility in complex environments where duplicate naming may occur.

The attribute used in an RDN is typically chosen based on schema conventions and organizational requirements. For user entries, the cn (common name) or uid (user ID) attributes are often used. For organizational units, the ou attribute is standard, and for domain components, dc is the preferred choice. Device entries might use the cn attribute to represent the device name, while groups often rely on cn as well. The choice of RDN attribute is influenced by the object class of the entry, which may specify required or recommended attributes suitable for use in RDNs.

The structure and syntax of DNs are governed by the LDAP and X.500 standards, which define how attribute-value pairs are formatted and concatenated. The DN syntax follows a comma-separated notation, where each RDN is separated by a comma, and attribute names and values are joined by an equals sign. Values containing special characters, such as commas, plus signs, or leading spaces, must be escaped with a backslash to prevent misinterpretation by the LDAP parser. For example, an entry with a common name of John Doe, Jr. would have its DN written as cn=John Doe, Jr.,ou=HR,dc=example,dc=com. Proper handling of special characters is essential for ensuring that DNs are correctly parsed and processed by clients and servers.

A key property of DNs is that they are immutable identifiers within the directory. If an entry's DN changes, it is effectively treated as a deletion of the original entry and the creation of a new one. For this reason, administrators must carefully consider DN design to avoid unnecessary renaming operations that could disrupt directory services. It is a common best practice to avoid including attributes in the DN that are likely to change, such as job titles or email addresses. Instead, stable attributes like uid or employee numbers are often favored for use in RDNs to maintain consistent DNs throughout the lifecycle of an entry.

When LDAP clients interact with the directory, they use DNs to perform operations such as search, bind, modify, and delete. For example, when binding to the directory to authenticate a user, the client provides the DN of the user entry along with a password. Similarly, search operations specify a base DN from which the search should begin, along with a scope that determines how deep into the tree the search should traverse. The ability to specify precise DNs allows for highly targeted queries, reducing server load and improving the performance of directory operations.

DNs are also critical in access control within LDAP. Many LDAP servers implement Access Control Lists (ACLs) based on the DN of the user or the DN of the entries being accessed. This allows administrators to apply fine-grained permissions, granting or restricting access to specific branches or entries within the DIT based on their DN. For instance, an administrator might allow users within ou=HR,dc=example,dc=com to view or modify entries only within their own organizational unit, enforcing a clear security boundary through DN-based rules.

In distributed LDAP environments, where multiple servers participate in a replication topology or federated directory system, DNs help ensure data integrity and consistency across systems. Each entry's DN serves as the authoritative reference point during replication operations, ensuring that data conflicts are avoided and that directory entries are accurately synchronized across all participating servers.

Additionally, the hierarchical nature of DNs and RDNs supports directory delegation and delegation of administrative control. Organizations can delegate the management of specific branches of the DIT to local administrators, empowering them to manage users, devices, and resources within their assigned subtree without affecting other parts of the directory. For example, an administrator responsible for ou=Sales,dc=example,dc=com can independently manage all entries within that subtree while having no access to other organizational units, such as ou=Engineering or ou=Finance.

In practice, designing an effective naming model using DNs and RDNs requires careful planning to ensure scalability, clarity, and ease of administration. The directory structure should reflect the logical organization of the business while providing enough flexibility to accommodate future growth and changes. A well-structured DN and RDN scheme simplifies directory management, enhances security through targeted access controls, and improves the overall usability of the directory service. Understanding the mechanics of Distinguished Names and Relative Distinguished Names is essential for building robust LDAP directories capable of supporting the complex identity and resource management needs of modern organizations.

Object Classes and Attributes

Object classes and attributes form the core components of the LDAP data model, defining how information is structured and stored within the directory. These two elements are inseparable from the way LDAP organizes its data, ensuring that every entry in the directory adheres to a predefined set of rules and maintains consistency across the system. Understanding object classes and attributes is essential for administrators who design directory schemas, developers who integrate LDAP into applications, and security professionals who rely on accurate identity data for access control.

An object class is a template that dictates the structural framework for directory entries. It defines what type of object the entry represents and specifies which attributes must or may be present. Every LDAP entry is an instance of at least one object class, which determines the permissible attributes for that entry. Object classes are defined within the LDAP schema, which acts as a catalog of rules and definitions used across the directory. Each object class has a name, an object identifier (OID), and a classification as either structural, auxiliary, or abstract. Structural object classes are the backbone of the directory structure, providing the required base for all entries. For instance, common structural object classes include organizationalUnit, which represents an organizational division, and inetOrgPerson, which represents a user or employee within an organization. Auxiliary object classes are designed to extend structural classes by providing additional, optional attributes that can be added to an entry without changing its fundamental type. For example, an entry for a user might use the posixAccount auxiliary object class to add attributes required for

UNIX-based systems. Abstract object classes are rarely used directly but serve as models for creating other object classes.

Each object class is defined by its set of mandatory and optional attributes. Mandatory attributes, also known as MUST attributes, are required when creating an entry of that object class. If any of these attributes are missing, the directory server will reject the entry as invalid. Optional attributes, referred to as MAY attributes, are not strictly required but can be included to provide additional information. Taking the inetOrgPerson object class as an example, it requires attributes like cn (common name) and sn (surname) while allowing optional attributes such as mail, telephoneNumber, and employeeNumber. This distinction ensures that all entries have a baseline level of information while also permitting flexibility to include additional details as needed.

Attributes themselves are individual pieces of data associated with directory entries. Each attribute is composed of a name and one or more values, depending on whether the attribute is single-valued or multi-valued. A single-valued attribute holds just one value, such as a uid (user ID), while a multi-valued attribute can store multiple values. For example, the member attribute used in group entries is often multi-valued, as a group typically contains multiple members. Attributes are typed according to specific syntaxes, which define the format of their values. Common syntaxes include Directory String, which supports text values; Integer, for numeric data; Boolean, for true or false values; and Distinguished Name, for references to other entries within the directory.

Attributes play a vital role in how LDAP entries are queried, managed, and integrated with applications. They contain the descriptive data that defines the identity and characteristics of directory objects. For example, a user entry might include attributes such as uid, cn, sn, mail, telephoneNumber, and userPassword. These attributes allow applications and administrators to perform operations like user authentication, email delivery, and directory lookups. Additionally, attributes are used in LDAP search filters, which specify criteria for locating entries that match certain conditions. A search filter could, for instance, request all entries where the department attribute equals

"Finance" and the title attribute equals "Manager."

LDAP attributes are defined globally within the schema and have specific rules regarding their use. Each attribute type is associated with an OID, a unique identifier that ensures consistency across different systems and organizations. Attributes also define matching rules, which determine how values are compared during directory operations. For example, the cn attribute typically uses a caseIgnoreMatch rule, allowing for case-insensitive comparisons, while attributes like userPassword may use octetStringMatch, which performs binary-level comparisons. These matching rules influence the behavior of search operations, equality tests, and other directory functions.

The extensibility of LDAP is largely due to the flexibility of its object class and attribute system. Organizations can define custom object classes and attributes to accommodate unique business needs. This is particularly useful when standard schema elements are insufficient for a given use case. For example, an organization might create a custom object class called customEmployee that includes attributes such as officeLocationCode or preferredLanguage, which are not part of the standard schema. Custom attributes are defined in the schema using LDIF files and then imported into the directory server. Each custom attribute must be assigned a unique OID to prevent conflicts with existing schema elements.

The relationship between object classes and attributes is hierarchical. A directory entry may inherit attributes from multiple object classes, as long as schema rules allow it. For instance, a user entry might simultaneously belong to the inetOrgPerson structural class and the posixAccount auxiliary class. This inheritance allows for modular and reusable schema design, where basic object classes define core attributes and auxiliary classes provide additional features or system-specific data. This flexibility ensures that LDAP directories can meet diverse requirements, from enterprise identity management to UNIX account provisioning or application-specific configurations.

LDAP object classes and attributes are also tightly integrated with access control mechanisms. Many LDAP servers allow administrators to define permissions at the attribute level. This means that while a user might have permission to read certain attributes, such as cn and mail, they may be restricted from viewing sensitive attributes like userPassword. This level of granularity enables organizations to protect sensitive data while still providing access to necessary information for applications and services.

Beyond user entries, object classes and attributes are used to model a variety of directory objects, including groups, roles, devices, printers, and services. For example, the groupOfNames object class is often used to create group entries that aggregate users or other entities via the member attribute, which contains a list of DNs. Similarly, the device object class might represent printers or network appliances, with attributes such as cn, serialNumber, and owner. This versatility allows LDAP directories to serve as comprehensive repositories for organizational data, supporting identity management, resource tracking, and service discovery within a single, unified framework.

The synergy between object classes and attributes gives LDAP its power and adaptability. The system provides a rigid yet extensible framework that ensures data integrity, facilitates interoperability, and supports complex organizational requirements. Understanding how object classes and attributes function, how they are defined in the schema, and how they relate to directory entries is essential for anyone responsible for designing, managing, or securing an LDAP environment. Whether working on a small internal directory or a large enterprise deployment, mastery of these fundamental elements is key to creating a robust and scalable directory service.

Setting Up an LDAP Server

Setting up an LDAP server is a fundamental task for organizations looking to implement centralized directory services to manage users, groups, devices, and other resources in a unified way. A properly configured LDAP server provides a scalable, secure, and efficient platform for storing and retrieving directory information across the network. The setup process involves selecting an LDAP server implementation, installing the necessary software, configuring the directory structure, defining access controls, and integrating security measures. While the specific steps may vary depending on the chosen LDAP server, the general principles and objectives are consistent across different platforms.

The first step in setting up an LDAP server is selecting the appropriate implementation based on the organization's requirements. OpenLDAP is one of the most widely used open-source LDAP server implementations, providing a flexible and highly configurable platform supported on many Unix-like systems. Other popular implementations include Microsoft Active Directory, which integrates LDAP with Kerberos and DNS for Windows-based environments, and commercial solutions like Red Hat Directory Server and Oracle Internet Directory. The choice depends on factors such as existing infrastructure, licensing preferences, integration needs, and administrative expertise.

Once the LDAP server software has been selected, the next step is installation. On Unix and Linux systems, OpenLDAP is often available directly through the package manager. Installing OpenLDAP typically involves installing the main server daemon, slapd, and associated utilities such as ldapadd, ldapmodify, and ldapsearch, which are essential for managing the directory. On Windows platforms, Active Directory Domain Services can be installed via the Server Manager, providing LDAP services as part of the broader Active Directory feature set. During installation, administrators should ensure that dependencies such as libraries for SSL/TLS encryption are also installed to support secure communications.

After the installation is complete, the LDAP server must be configured to define the initial directory structure and operational parameters. This configuration is typically handled through a configuration backend or file, such as slapd.conf or cn=config in OpenLDAP, or through graphical tools in the case of Active Directory. A key part of this configuration is establishing the directory's suffix, which defines the root of the Directory Information Tree. For instance, an organization with the domain example.com might use dc=example,dc=com as the directory suffix. This becomes the base of the directory hierarchy under which all subsequent entries will reside.

Next, the directory's schema must be reviewed and, if necessary, extended to meet the organization's data requirements. By default,

LDAP servers come with a set of core schema files that include widely used object classes and attributes, such as inetOrgPerson, organizationalUnit, and groupOfNames. If the organization needs to store custom data fields, administrators may create custom schema definitions to introduce new object classes and attributes tailored to specific applications or business processes. Careful schema design is critical, as it directly affects how data is structured and accessed within the directory.

With the schema in place, administrators can begin populating the directory with initial data. This is commonly done using LDIF (LDAP Data Interchange Format) files, which provide a text-based representation of directory entries. Using the ldapadd command in OpenLDAP or equivalent tools in other implementations, administrators can import users, organizational units, and groups into the directory. For example, an LDIF file might define an organizational unit with an entry such as dn: ou=HR,dc=example,dc=com followed by its associated attributes. Entries for users might follow with their own distinguished names, object classes, and attribute sets.

At this stage, it is crucial to configure access controls to ensure that directory data is properly secured. LDAP servers implement Access Control Lists (ACLs) that specify which users or groups are permitted to perform specific operations on directory entries. ACLs can be configured at various levels, from granting anonymous read access to public information to enforcing strict restrictions on sensitive attributes like user passwords. For example, administrators might configure the directory to allow users to read their own entries but restrict write access to administrators only. This granular access control helps prevent unauthorized modifications and protects sensitive information.

Securing the LDAP server also involves configuring encryption to protect data in transit. LDAP supports encryption via SSL/TLS, which secures communications between clients and the server against eavesdropping and tampering. Configuring SSL/TLS requires the generation of digital certificates and private keys, which can be self-signed for internal use or obtained from a trusted certificate authority for broader trust. Once SSL/TLS is enabled, LDAP clients connect to the server using LDAPS, the LDAP protocol over a secure connection, typically on port 636.

Additional security measures include enforcing strong authentication methods. LDAP supports a range of authentication mechanisms, from anonymous binds and simple username/password authentication to more advanced methods such as SASL (Simple Authentication and Security Layer) integrations with external authentication services like Kerberos. For production environments, it is recommended to avoid anonymous binds and to implement multi-factor authentication or integrate with enterprise authentication systems to strengthen identity verification processes.

Once security policies are in place, administrators can further optimize the LDAP server by configuring indexing for frequently queried attributes. Indexing improves search performance by reducing the time required to locate specific entries within large directories. Commonly indexed attributes include uid, cn, and mail, which are frequently used as search criteria in directory lookups.

Finally, administrators should implement monitoring and maintenance procedures to ensure the ongoing health of the LDAP server. Monitoring tools can track metrics such as query response times, connection counts, and resource utilization. Regular backups of the directory data should also be scheduled to mitigate the risk of data loss due to system failures or accidental deletions. In OpenLDAP, backups are often created by exporting the entire directory to an LDIF file using the slapcat utility.

Throughout the setup process, it is important to validate the LDAP server's functionality by performing test operations using client tools such as ldapsearch and ldapwhoami. These tests verify that the server is correctly processing queries, enforcing access controls, and securing data transmissions. Additional integration tests may be needed to confirm compatibility with external systems, such as authentication services, email platforms, or business applications that rely on directory data.

Setting up an LDAP server is not only about getting the software running but also about designing a secure, scalable, and manageable directory service that will support the organization's operational needs. Each step, from schema configuration to access control and encryption, contributes to building a reliable foundation for identity and resource management. A well-deployed LDAP server becomes a central hub in the IT infrastructure, enabling streamlined user management, secure authentication, and centralized resource directory services.

LDAP Client Tools and Utilities

LDAP client tools and utilities are essential for interacting with an LDAP directory, enabling administrators, developers, and automated systems to perform a variety of operations such as searching, modifying, adding, and deleting directory entries. These tools provide the interface between users or applications and the LDAP server, allowing them to query and manage directory data according to their roles and permissions. Understanding how these utilities work is crucial for both day-to-day administrative tasks and for integrating LDAP into larger systems and workflows.

One of the most widely used LDAP client utilities is ldapsearch. This command-line tool allows users to perform searches against the directory using specified search filters, base distinguished names, and scopes. ldapsearch is typically bundled with LDAP server distributions such as OpenLDAP, but it can also be installed independently for client-side operations. The tool is invaluable for troubleshooting and auditing, as it provides raw access to directory queries and outputs results in a clear, text-based format. By specifying the search base, filter, and desired attributes, administrators can quickly extract relevant information from the directory. For instance, running ldapsearch with a filter like (uid=jdoe) allows an administrator to retrieve all the attributes associated with a user identified by the uid jdoe.

Another critical tool is ldapadd, which is used to create new entries in the LDAP directory. ldapadd takes input from an LDIF (LDAP Data Interchange Format) file, which describes one or more directory entries in a structured, text-based syntax. The tool reads the LDIF data and sends it to the server to be processed as add operations. This utility is often used when populating a new directory for the first time, when migrating data from another directory system, or when automating user onboarding processes. ldapadd provides feedback during execution, reporting successful operations as well as errors, such as schema violations or access control restrictions.

Complementing ldapadd is ldapmodify, a utility designed to modify existing entries within the directory. Like ldapadd, ldapmodify accepts LDIF input, but instead of creating new entries, it applies changes to existing objects. The tool supports operations such as adding new attributes, replacing attribute values, or deleting attributes from an entry. For example, if an administrator needs to update the telephone number for a user, ldapmodify can be used with an LDIF file that specifies the DN of the user and the replacement value for the telephoneNumber attribute. ldapmodify is particularly useful for bulk updates or for automating routine maintenance tasks such as updating department codes or job titles across multiple user entries.

ldapdelete is another important utility that allows administrators to remove entries from the directory. This tool is used with caution, as deletions are immediate and, unless the directory is configured with recycle bin features or shadow copies, irreversible. To delete an entry, the administrator specifies the DN of the object to be removed, and the tool sends the request to the LDAP server for execution. ldapdelete can be used interactively or as part of scripted operations where entries need to be cleaned up as part of offboarding processes or directory maintenance tasks.

In addition to these core command-line utilities, LDAP client tools also include graphical interfaces that simplify directory management for users who prefer a visual approach. One widely used graphical tool is Apache Directory Studio, an Eclipse-based LDAP browser and directory client that provides a comprehensive interface for browsing, editing, and managing LDAP directories. Apache Directory Studio supports connecting to multiple LDAP servers, viewing the directory tree, editing entries, managing schema definitions, and performing search operations through a user-friendly graphical environment. This tool is particularly valuable for administrators who need to perform complex operations without writing long command-line queries or LDIF files manually.

Web-based LDAP clients also play an important role in directory management. Applications such as phpLDAPadmin and LDAP Account Manager provide browser-based interfaces that allow administrators to perform common directory tasks from any system with web access. These tools typically include features such as entry creation and modification, group membership management, password resets, and bulk user imports. By providing role-based access and customizable templates, web-based LDAP clients streamline many administrative workflows and reduce the likelihood of configuration errors.

For developers and automation engineers, LDAP libraries and APIs serve as client-side components for integrating LDAP operations into custom applications and scripts. Libraries such as python-ldap for Python, Net::LDAP for Perl, and the JNDI (Java Naming and Directory Interface) API for Java provide programmatic access to LDAP directories. These libraries enable applications to authenticate users, retrieve directory data, and automate directory modifications as part of larger workflows. For example, a Python script might use python-ldap to automatically provision new employees in the directory by creating user entries and assigning group memberships based on data from an HR system.

Beyond interactive tools and programming libraries, system-level utilities often interact with LDAP servers as part of operating system authentication and access control mechanisms. Many Unix-like systems can be configured to use LDAP as a central authentication source via tools such as nslcd or SSSD. These services integrate LDAP queries directly into the system's Pluggable Authentication Modules (PAM) and Name Service Switch (NSS) frameworks, allowing LDAP users to log in to servers and workstations as if their accounts were local. These utilities handle operations such as retrieving user attributes, validating passwords, and resolving group memberships transparently to the end user.

Network administrators and security professionals often rely on LDAP client tools to audit directory contents, test authentication scenarios, and diagnose performance issues. Tools like ldapwhoami can be used to verify the identity under which a client is authenticated to the directory, which is helpful when testing access control policies and permissions. Similarly, ldapcompare is a utility that checks whether a specified attribute of an entry matches a given value, assisting in validation workflows and troubleshooting.

The functionality of LDAP client tools is also critical in the context of security and compliance. Regular audits using tools like ldapsearch can help identify unauthorized modifications, orphaned accounts, or policy violations within the directory. Automation scripts built on top of LDAP client libraries can enforce security policies by detecting anomalies or automatically deactivating accounts that no longer meet compliance requirements.

LDAP client tools and utilities form a vital ecosystem around the directory server, enabling seamless interaction with the directory's data. Whether performing one-time administrative tasks, automating recurring processes, integrating LDAP into applications, or troubleshooting operational issues, these tools provide the necessary functionality to manage and leverage LDAP directories effectively. Mastery of both command-line and graphical LDAP clients enhances an administrator's ability to maintain a reliable and secure directory service while supporting the organization's broader identity and access management objectives.

Performing LDAP Searches

Performing LDAP searches is one of the most fundamental and frequent operations when working with directory services. The LDAP protocol is highly optimized for reading data, making search operations a core feature of every LDAP-enabled environment. Users, administrators, and applications rely on searches to retrieve directory entries based on specific criteria, whether to authenticate users, display user profiles, or manage resources like groups, devices, and services. Understanding how LDAP search operations work is critical to maximizing directory performance, accuracy, and efficiency.

Every LDAP search begins with three essential components: the base Distinguished Name (DN), the search scope, and the search filter. The base DN specifies the entry within the Directory Information Tree from which the search will begin. This can be any node within the tree, from the root entry (such as dc=example,dc=com) to a more specific branch like ou=HR,dc=example,dc=com or even a single user entry like cn=John Smith,ou=HR,dc=example,dc=com. The base DN acts as the anchor point for the search, limiting where the LDAP server looks for matching entries. Specifying the correct base DN is key to optimizing search efficiency, as narrowing the search to the relevant subtree reduces processing time and server load.

The second component of the search is the scope, which defines how deep into the directory tree the search should go, starting from the base DN. LDAP supports three standard scopes: base, one-level, and subtree. A base scope limits the search to the base DN itself and is used to retrieve a single entry. A one-level scope searches all entries that are immediate children of the base DN but does not include the base DN itself or any deeper descendants. This scope is often used to list all users in a specific organizational unit without searching through sub-organizations. The subtree scope, which is the most expansive, searches the base DN and all of its descendants, regardless of depth. Subtree searches are useful when looking for entries scattered across multiple levels of the directory tree, but they can be resource-intensive if not properly filtered.

The third critical element is the search filter, which specifies the conditions that directory entries must meet to be included in the search results. LDAP search filters follow a specific syntax based on parentheses, attribute names, operators, and values. The most common operator is the equality operator, represented by an equals sign. For example, the filter (uid=jdoe) searches for entries where the uid attribute equals jdoe. Filters can also use the presence operator, represented by an asterisk, to find entries where an attribute is present, such as (mail=*), which would return all entries with a mail attribute.

LDAP filters support logical operators to combine multiple conditions. The AND operator is represented by an ampersand within the filter, and the OR operator by a pipe symbol. For example, a filter like (&(department=Sales)(title=Manager)) returns entries where both the department equals Sales and the title equals Manager. Conversely, a filter like (|(department=Sales)(department=Marketing)) returns entries from either the Sales or Marketing departments. The NOT operator, represented by an exclamation mark, allows for the exclusion of entries matching a particular condition, such as (!(status=inactive)), which excludes entries marked as inactive.

In addition to logical operators, filters can include substring matches, where partial values are specified using asterisks as wildcards. For example, (cn=John*) matches all entries where the common name starts with John, such as John Smith or Johnny Adams. More complex substring filters like (cn=*Smith) match entries where the common name ends with Smith, while (cn=ohn) matches entries where the letters "ohn" appear anywhere within the common name.

The LDAP search request also includes a list of attributes to be returned as part of the search results. This allows clients to control how much data is retrieved from the server. For example, specifying only cn and mail as requested attributes ensures that the search response does not include unnecessary attributes like telephoneNumber or employeeNumber. This selective retrieval is important for improving search performance and reducing network bandwidth usage. Alternatively, using an asterisk in the attributes list retrieves all user-defined attributes, while the plus sign returns operational attributes such as entryUUID or createTimestamp, which are metadata maintained by the server.

Executing an LDAP search requires binding to the server with appropriate credentials unless anonymous access is permitted. The bind operation establishes the session's identity and determines which entries the client is authorized to access based on Access Control Lists (ACLs) defined on the LDAP server. Once authenticated, the client submits the search request, and the server processes it according to the specified base DN, scope, and filter. The server then returns a set of matching entries, each with its requested attributes, or an empty result if no matches are found.

On the command line, tools like ldapsearch are commonly used to perform LDAP search operations. An administrator might issue a command such as ldapsearch -x -b "ou=Engineering,dc=example,dc=com" "(title=Developer)" cn mail, which searches for entries in the Engineering organizational unit with the title Developer and returns their common names and email addresses. The -x flag indicates simple authentication, and the -b flag specifies the base DN. Similar search requests can be performed using graphical LDAP clients like Apache Directory Studio, where search filters, scopes, and attributes are entered into visual forms rather than typed on the command line.

LDAP search operations are also integrated into many applications and services that rely on directories for authentication and user management. Web applications might use LDAP searches to validate login credentials, retrieve user profiles, or enforce group membership requirements. Mail servers often use directory searches to resolve recipient addresses, while HR systems might pull organizational data from the LDAP directory to populate internal databases.

To ensure search efficiency, LDAP administrators often configure attribute indexing on the server side. Indexing frequently queried attributes such as uid, cn, and mail significantly reduces search latency, especially in large directories. Without indexing, the server may perform full tree scans to find matching entries, which can lead to performance bottlenecks.

LDAP search operations also support paged results control, an extension that allows large result sets to be broken into manageable pages. This is particularly useful when an application needs to retrieve thousands of entries but must do so incrementally to avoid timeouts or memory issues on the client or server. Paged searches provide a mechanism to receive results in chunks while maintaining session state between requests.

Search operations are at the heart of every interaction with an LDAP directory, enabling efficient retrieval of critical identity and resource data. Mastering search syntax, scope selection, and filter design empowers administrators and developers to build responsive, scalable, and secure directory services that meet the demands of modern IT environments. Whether troubleshooting directory issues, building integrations, or managing daily operations, LDAP searches are an indispensable tool in the toolkit of anyone working with directory services.

LDAP Search Filters Explained

LDAP search filters are a fundamental part of how clients query directory data. They allow precise targeting of entries within the directory by specifying conditions that entries must meet to be included in the search results. The power and flexibility of LDAP filters come from their ability to combine simple comparisons, logical operations, and pattern matching within a compact and structured syntax. Filters can be as simple as finding a user by username or as complex as locating all users who belong to multiple groups and meet several attribute criteria simultaneously. Understanding how to write and optimize LDAP search filters is essential for efficient directory management and integration with applications.

The basic structure of an LDAP search filter consists of an attribute, an operator, and a value, all enclosed in parentheses. The most common operator is the equality operator, represented by the equals sign. A simple example of this is (uid=jdoe), which searches for entries where the uid attribute is exactly equal to the value jdoe. This type of filter is often used in authentication workflows, where applications search the directory for a user by their unique identifier. The attribute name must correspond to a valid attribute defined in the directory's schema, and the value must follow the attribute's defined syntax.

Beyond equality, LDAP filters also support presence filters, where the goal is to identify entries that contain a specific attribute, regardless of its value. A presence filter uses an asterisk as a wildcard for the value, as in (mail=), which matches all entries that have a mail attribute defined. Presence filters are useful for finding incomplete records or identifying entries missing certain data. For example, searching for (!(telephoneNumber=)) would return entries where the telephoneNumber attribute is absent, which could indicate missing or incomplete user profiles.

LDAP filters are also capable of performing substring matches, where the asterisk is used within the value to match partial strings. A filter like (cn=John*) matches entries where the cn attribute begins with John, such as John Smith or Johnny Davis. A filter such as (cn=*Smith) matches entries ending with Smith, while (cn=ohn) would match any entry where the substring "ohn" appears anywhere within the common name. Substring filters are particularly helpful in user search interfaces, where users might only know part of a name or an incomplete identifier.

In addition to simple comparisons, LDAP search filters support complex logic through the use of logical operators. The AND operator is represented by an ampersand and allows the combination of multiple conditions that must all be true for an entry to match. An example of an AND filter is (&(department=Engineering)(title=Manager)), which matches entries where the department attribute equals Engineering and the title attribute equals Manager. The OR operator, represented by a pipe symbol, matches entries where at least one condition is true. A filter like (|(department=Sales)(department=Marketing)) retrieves entries belonging to either the Sales or Marketing departments.

The NOT operator is represented by an exclamation mark and is used to exclude entries matching a specified condition. For example, (!(status=inactive)) will exclude all entries where the status attribute is set to inactive. NOT filters are often combined with AND or OR filters to create more refined queries. For instance, a filter such as (&(department=Engineering)(!(status=inactive))) will return all active employees in the Engineering department by excluding those marked as inactive.

LDAP search filters can be nested to create highly specific queries. Filters inside other filters enable the construction of complex logic trees that can evaluate multiple layers of conditions. For example, a nested filter like (&(|(department=Engineering)(department=IT))(!(status=inactive))) will return entries from either the Engineering or IT departments while excluding those who are inactive. This ability to nest AND, OR, and NOT conditions provides LDAP clients with powerful search capabilities to handle sophisticated directory queries.

LDAP filters also support comparison operators beyond simple equality. The greater than or equal to operator is represented by >= and is used to find entries where an attribute's value is greater than or equal to the specified value, assuming the attribute's syntax supports ordering, such as integers or dates. For example, (employeeNumber>=1000) might return all employees with an ID of 1000 or higher. Similarly, the less than or equal to operator, represented by <=, can be used to find entries with attribute values less than or equal to the specified value, such as (loginCount<=5) to locate users who have logged in five times or fewer.

Filters are also extensible through the use of extensible match rules, allowing searches to apply specific matching rules beyond the default schema-defined behavior. For instance, an extensible match filter might specify a case-insensitive or language-specific matching rule explicitly. An example would be (cn:caseExactMatch:=John Doe), which enforces a case-sensitive match against the cn attribute. Extensible match filters are less common in everyday administration but are valuable in advanced scenarios where default matching behavior does not meet specific application requirements.

In LDAP search operations, the filter plays a significant role in determining performance. Poorly designed filters can cause excessive server load, especially in large directories with thousands or millions of entries. To optimize searches, administrators often configure indexing on frequently queried attributes. When an attribute like uid, cn, or mail is indexed, the server can quickly locate matching entries without scanning the entire directory. Search filters should also be as specific as possible, avoiding unbounded subtree searches combined with broad filters like (objectClass=*) unless necessary.

Filters are integral to access control scenarios as well. Some LDAP servers implement dynamic group membership, where a group's members are determined by a search filter rather than a static list of DNs. This allows administrators to define group membership based on attributes. For example, a dynamic group might include all entries where (department=HR) or all users with the status of active. Dynamic filters make group management more automated and adaptable to changes in directory data.

Filters are also used extensively in applications that integrate with LDAP directories. When an application needs to authenticate a user, it typically performs a search using a filter like (uid=username) to locate the user's DN before attempting a bind operation. Applications that implement role-based access control may use filters to verify group membership by searching for entries with a member attribute containing the user's DN. Similarly, self-service portals might allow users to search for their colleagues by partial name or department, relying on LDAP substring and logical filters to power the search functionality.

The syntax of LDAP search filters is standardized, ensuring compatibility across different LDAP servers and client libraries. However, variations in schema design and attribute availability mean that filters must be tailored to the specific directory in use. For instance, one organization might use uid as the unique identifier for users, while another uses sAMAccountName or employeeID. Understanding the directory's schema is essential for writing effective filters that return accurate results.

LDAP search filters are one of the most powerful aspects of the protocol, enabling highly granular and efficient querying of directory data. Mastering filter syntax and logic provides administrators and developers with the ability to create fast, precise, and secure directory queries suited to a wide range of operational and application needs. Whether performing simple user lookups or constructing complex conditional searches, LDAP filters are an indispensable tool for unlocking the full potential of the directory service.

Modifying Directory Entries

Modifying directory entries in LDAP is a core administrative task that allows administrators and applications to update, extend, or correct information stored in the directory. Since directories are dynamic systems where user details, organizational structures, and resource records are constantly evolving, modification operations are vital for keeping the directory current and aligned with the organization's needs. LDAP provides a structured and standardized approach to modifying entries through its protocol operations, ensuring that changes are executed securely, consistently, and according to schema constraints.

At its core, the LDAP modify operation is designed to alter one or more attributes of an existing directory entry. Modifications can include adding new attributes to an entry, deleting existing attributes, or replacing attribute values. Each modification request is performed against a specific entry identified by its Distinguished Name (DN), which uniquely locates the entry within the Directory Information Tree (DIT). The modify operation does not affect the DN itself; changes to an entry's DN, such as moving it to a different branch or renaming it, require a separate operation called modify DN or modrdn.

To perform a modification, an LDAP client such as ldapmodify is used to submit a request to the directory server. The request specifies the target DN and a series of modification instructions, each indicating the type of change and the attribute(s) involved. Modification instructions follow a specific structure: they begin with an action keyword such as add, delete, or replace, followed by the attribute name and associated values. These operations can be combined within a single request, allowing for multiple changes to be made to the same entry in one atomic transaction.

The add operation is used to introduce new attributes to an entry or to add new values to a multi-valued attribute. For example, if a user entry does not currently have a telephoneNumber attribute, an add operation can be used to insert this attribute along with its value. If the attribute is multi-valued, such as mail or memberOf, the add operation can append additional values without overwriting existing ones. However, attempting to add an attribute that already exists as single-valued will typically result in an error unless the directory schema allows multiple values.

The delete operation removes an attribute entirely from an entry or deletes specific values from a multi-valued attribute. Deleting an entire attribute is useful for cleaning up obsolete or incorrect data, such as removing an outdated pagerNumber attribute. When targeting multi-valued attributes, the delete operation can specify the exact value to be removed. For instance, removing a specific email address from the mail attribute without affecting other addresses associated with the same user.

The replace operation is used to overwrite the values of an existing attribute. It first removes all current values of the attribute and then assigns the new value(s) provided in the request. The replace operation is ideal for updating attributes like job titles, office locations, or manager relationships, where the attribute should only have a single, current value. It is important to ensure that replace operations comply with the attribute's defined syntax and that required attributes specified by the object class are not inadvertently removed during the update.

All modify operations must adhere to the rules defined in the LDAP schema. The schema enforces which attributes are allowed or mandatory based on the object class associated with the entry. For example, an entry using the inetOrgPerson object class must include attributes such as cn (common name) and sn (surname), and attempts to delete these required attributes will be rejected by the server. Similarly, adding an attribute not permitted by the entry's object class without first extending the schema will result in an error.

LDAP modify operations require proper authentication and authorization. The server enforces access controls through Access Control Lists (ACLs) or equivalent mechanisms to ensure that only authorized users can modify specific entries or attributes. For example, a regular user may be permitted to update personal details such as their phone number or home address, but only administrators might be allowed to change sensitive attributes like userPassword or modify membership of privileged groups. The bind DN used during the modification process determines the client's access level and dictates which operations can be performed successfully.

LDAP modifications can be executed using command-line tools such as ldapmodify or through graphical LDAP clients like Apache Directory Studio. When using ldapmodify, administrators typically provide the modification instructions in an LDIF (LDAP Data Interchange Format) file. This file outlines the DN of the entry and the list of changes to be applied. For example, an LDIF snippet might include dn: cn=John Doe,ou=HR,dc=example,dc=com followed by a replace operation for the title attribute to update the user's job title. Executing ldapmodify with this file will send the modification request to the server, which processes the changes atomically.

Applications and scripts often perform LDAP modifications programmatically using LDAP libraries such as python-ldap for Python or JNDI for Java. These libraries expose modify functions that accept the DN of the target entry and a list of operations to execute. This allows developers to automate routine updates such as synchronizing LDAP with external systems like HR databases or customer relationship management platforms. For example, an HR system might trigger a script to automatically update a user's department and manager attributes in the LDAP directory whenever an employee is promoted or transferred internally.

Modifications are also a key part of self-service portals where users can update their own information. Web-based applications that interface with LDAP directories often provide forms where users can edit attributes like mobile phone numbers, office locations, or emergency contact details. Behind the scenes, these updates are performed through modify operations sent to the directory server, subject to access control rules defined by the administrators.

Modifying directory entries plays an essential role in workflows like onboarding, offboarding, and internal transfers. During onboarding, user accounts are often created with minimal required information and then enriched over time with additional attributes such as group memberships, department codes, or SSH public keys. During offboarding, modify operations might deactivate accounts by setting attributes like loginShell to /sbin/nologin or changing user status attributes to inactive. When employees move between departments, modify operations ensure that directory entries are updated to reflect new organizational structures, responsibilities, and reporting lines.

Proper logging and auditing of LDAP modifications are essential for maintaining directory integrity and supporting compliance requirements. Most LDAP servers provide detailed logs of modify operations, capturing information such as the bind DN performing the change, the attributes modified, and timestamps for each operation. This audit trail is valuable for troubleshooting, security investigations, and demonstrating adherence to regulatory standards in industries where data governance is critical.

Ultimately, the ability to modify directory entries efficiently and securely is foundational to the success of any LDAP deployment. Whether through manual updates, automation scripts, or application integrations, the modify operation ensures that directory data remains accurate, complete, and reflective of the organization's current state. By mastering the modification process, administrators can build a flexible and responsive directory service that supports both operational needs and long-term scalability.

Adding and Deleting Entries

Adding and deleting entries are two of the most common and essential operations in LDAP directory management. These actions form the foundation of directory administration, as organizations must frequently create new directory objects to reflect onboarding processes and remove entries when users, groups, or resources are decommissioned. The ability to accurately and securely add and delete entries ensures that the directory remains a reliable and up-to-date repository of information, supporting identity management, authentication, and access control processes across the organization.

To add an entry in an LDAP directory, the administrator or application must provide a complete and valid definition of the new object. Each entry is defined by its Distinguished Name, or DN, which identifies its unique position within the Directory Information Tree. The DN is composed of one or more Relative Distinguished Names that locate the entry relative to its parent node. For example, a new user entry might have a DN such as cn=Alice Johnson,ou=Marketing,dc=example,dc=com, which indicates that Alice Johnson will be placed under the Marketing organizational unit within the directory structure.

When adding an entry, the object class is specified to define the type of the entry and the set of required and optional attributes it must contain. An object class such as inetOrgPerson is commonly used for user entries, while organizationalUnit is used for departmental or organizational branches. The schema enforces the rules associated with the object class. For instance, an inetOrgPerson entry must include attributes like cn (common name) and sn (surname), while optional attributes may include mail, telephoneNumber, and employeeNumber. The administrator must ensure that all mandatory attributes are present when creating the entry, or the LDAP server will reject the add request due to schema violations.

The add operation is typically executed using tools such as ldapadd, which reads entries from an LDIF (LDAP Data Interchange Format) file and submits them to the directory server. The LDIF file provides a structured text representation of one or more directory entries, specifying their DN, object classes, and attribute values. A sample LDIF entry for a new user might include the DN, objectClass declarations, and attributes like uid, mail, and userPassword. Once the ldapadd command is executed, the server validates the entry, applies schema checks, and, if successful, adds the entry to the directory.

LDAP entries can also be added programmatically using client libraries such as python-ldap for Python, UnboundID SDK for Java, or Net::LDAP for Perl. These libraries provide APIs for constructing and submitting add requests, making it easy to integrate LDAP entry creation into automation workflows or custom applications. For example, a human resources system could automatically create new employee entries in the LDAP directory when new hires are added to the HR database.

Adding entries is not limited to user objects. LDAP directories also store entries for groups, devices, services, and other resources. For example, a group entry might be created using the groupOfNames object class, which includes attributes like cn for the group name and member attributes listing the DNs of its members. Device entries might use the device object class and include attributes such as cn, serialNumber, and owner.

The delete operation in LDAP is used to remove directory entries. The ldapdelete utility is commonly used for this task, requiring only the DN of the entry to be removed. Deleting an entry removes it from the directory tree, and once deleted, the entry is no longer retrievable unless recovery mechanisms like backups or recycle bin features are in place. Deleting entries must be approached with caution, especially in production environments, to avoid accidental loss of important data or disruption of dependent services.

When an entry is deleted, the LDAP server enforces rules to ensure directory integrity. For instance, an entry cannot be deleted if it has child entries unless a recursive delete feature is explicitly invoked, which is not supported natively in many LDAP servers. To delete an entire subtree, administrators must first delete all subordinate entries before removing the parent entry. This prevents accidental deletion of entire branches of the directory tree, which could have wide-reaching effects on organizational systems.

Deleting entries also has implications for relationships and dependencies within the directory. For example, removing a user entry that is a member of one or more groups will leave those group entries referencing a non-existent DN unless group cleanup procedures are implemented. Similarly, deleting an entry referenced by other objects via attributes like manager or owner may result in dangling references. For this reason, directory cleanup processes often include steps to update or remove such references when an entry is deleted.

In addition to manual deletions, organizations often automate the deletion process using scripts or integrated systems. For instance, a deprovisioning workflow might automatically remove an employee's LDAP entry when they leave the company, based on data received from an HR or identity management system. Automation ensures that offboarding processes are executed consistently and reduces the risk of leaving inactive or orphaned entries in the directory.

While ldapdelete is a standard command-line tool for entry removal, graphical LDAP clients like Apache Directory Studio provide user-friendly interfaces for deleting entries. Administrators can browse the directory tree, select an entry, and delete it with a right-click action. These tools often include confirmation prompts and safeguards to prevent accidental deletions. Some graphical clients also offer batch deletion features, where multiple entries can be selected and removed simultaneously.

For security and compliance purposes, it is crucial to log add and delete operations in the LDAP server's audit logs. These logs provide a record of who performed the operation, when it was executed, and what DN was affected. Auditing helps organizations meet regulatory requirements and supports forensic analysis if unauthorized or accidental changes are suspected.

In some environments, rather than deleting user entries immediately, organizations implement soft-deletion mechanisms by modifying an attribute such as accountStatus or isActive to indicate that the entry is disabled. This approach preserves historical data and allows for easier reactivation of accounts if needed. Later, periodic cleanup scripts may permanently remove entries marked as inactive for a specified retention period.

Both adding and deleting entries are essential actions in the lifecycle of directory management. They enable administrators to reflect organizational changes, enforce data accuracy, and maintain a lean and efficient directory service. These operations must be carried out with attention to schema requirements, access control policies, and the broader operational context to avoid inconsistencies or disruptions. Mastering these functions equips administrators and developers with the tools to maintain a dynamic and well-governed LDAP environment.

LDAP Bind Operations

LDAP bind operations are the mechanism by which a client authenticates to an LDAP directory server, establishing the identity under which subsequent directory requests will be executed. The bind operation is a foundational component of the LDAP protocol, governing the security context for every interaction between a client and the directory. Without binding, an LDAP client cannot perform meaningful operations, as the directory must first determine the client's identity and verify that it has the necessary permissions to access or manipulate data. The bind process is therefore critical for enforcing security policies, protecting sensitive information, and enabling controlled access to directory resources.

The simplest form of bind operation is the anonymous bind. In this scenario, a client connects to the LDAP server without supplying any credentials. An anonymous bind is useful for public directories where certain data, such as a corporate phone book or public user profiles, is made available to anyone without requiring authentication. However, anonymous binds are rarely used in modern production environments due to the inherent security risks associated with unauthenticated access. Most organizations restrict or completely disable anonymous binds to ensure that only authenticated users can query the directory.

A more common and secure method is the simple bind operation. In a simple bind, the client provides a Distinguished Name and a password to authenticate to the LDAP server. The DN identifies the user account within the directory, while the password is verified by the server to confirm the client's identity. A successful simple bind establishes an authenticated session under the context of the provided DN. This form of authentication is widely supported and easy to implement, making it the default method for many LDAP integrations. However, simple bind operations transmit the password in clear text unless the LDAP session is secured using SSL/TLS encryption. To mitigate this risk, best practices dictate that simple binds should always be performed over LDAPS or StartTLS connections to protect credentials from eavesdropping during transit.

The bind operation process begins when the client issues a bind request to the LDAP server. The request includes the authentication method, the bind DN, and any associated credentials. Upon receiving the request, the server attempts to locate the bind DN within the Directory Information Tree and validate the credentials provided. If the DN does not exist or the credentials are invalid, the server returns an error, and the client's session remains unauthenticated. If the authentication is successful, the server returns a success response, and the session is marked as bound, allowing the client to proceed with additional LDAP operations such as search, modify, or delete, subject to the permissions granted to the authenticated identity.

LDAP also supports more advanced bind methods through the Simple Authentication and Security Layer, or SASL, framework. SASL provides a pluggable authentication mechanism that enables LDAP servers and clients to negotiate various authentication protocols. Common SASL mechanisms include DIGEST-MD5, GSSAPI for Kerberos-based authentication, and EXTERNAL for using client-side TLS certificates. The advantage of SASL mechanisms is that they offer stronger security features, such as mutual authentication, password hashing, and support for single sign-on environments. For example, in an organization that uses Kerberos, the GSSAPI mechanism allows LDAP clients to bind using Kerberos tickets instead of transmitting passwords, enhancing both security and user convenience.

In some environments, the LDAP proxy authorization control is used in conjunction with SASL binds to allow one user to act on behalf of another. This is particularly useful for applications and services that need to perform directory operations under the context of end users without having access to their actual credentials. The proxy authorization control enables the authenticated service to specify the authorization identity for each request, as long as the service has been granted the necessary permissions to do so.

Bind operations also play a key role in managing session state and access control. The permissions associated with the bound DN determine what parts of the directory the client can access and which operations are permitted. For example, a client bound as a regular user might be able to read its own attributes and perform password changes but would be restricted from modifying other users' data or accessing sensitive entries such as administrative accounts. Conversely, a client bound as an LDAP administrator or service account may have broader permissions, including the ability to manage users, groups, and directory schema elements. LDAP Access Control Lists (ACLs) are enforced based on the identity established during the bind operation, ensuring that security policies are consistently applied across all directory interactions.

It is also possible to perform an LDAP bind using credentials stored in external identity providers or authentication systems. Many organizations integrate LDAP with centralized identity management solutions, such as Active Directory or external Kerberos realms, to streamline authentication processes. In these setups, the LDAP server delegates credential verification to the external system while still managing directory data internally. This approach provides a single point of authentication across multiple services and applications, improving security and reducing administrative overhead.

When developing LDAP-enabled applications, it is crucial to handle bind operations carefully to avoid security risks and performance issues. Applications should always use secure connections for binds, avoid hardcoding credentials, and implement proper error handling to detect and respond to bind failures. Some applications implement connection pooling, where a pool of pre-authenticated connections is maintained to reduce the overhead associated with frequent bind and unbind cycles. This approach is common in high-traffic environments where applications issue thousands of LDAP queries per hour.

From an auditing perspective, LDAP bind operations are often logged by the directory server, providing a record of authentication attempts, including the bind DN, the client's IP address, and the result of each bind request. These logs are invaluable for monitoring directory usage, detecting unauthorized access attempts, and troubleshooting authentication issues. In environments subject to regulatory compliance, detailed bind logs may be required to demonstrate adherence to security policies and auditing standards.

In the context of high-availability architectures, LDAP servers configured in a load-balanced or replicated setup handle bind operations across multiple instances to ensure redundancy and fault tolerance. When a client initiates a bind, the load balancer routes the request to an available LDAP server, which then processes the authentication request as usual. This ensures that bind operations remain functional even during server outages or network disruptions.

LDAP bind operations serve as the gateway to secure and controlled access to directory services. Whether performed as anonymous, simple, or SASL binds, the bind step defines the identity and permissions of every LDAP session. For administrators, developers, and security professionals, understanding how bind operations work is essential to building secure directory integrations, enforcing effective access controls, and maintaining the integrity of the LDAP environment. Properly executed bind processes ensure that only trusted users and applications can interact with directory data, forming the first line of defense in any identity management infrastructure.

LDAP Authentication Methods

LDAP authentication methods are central to securing directory services and ensuring that only authorized users and applications can access or modify directory data. As directories frequently store sensitive information such as user credentials, organizational structures, and access control policies, proper authentication mechanisms are crucial for maintaining the integrity and confidentiality of the system. LDAP supports a variety of authentication methods, ranging from simple approaches suitable for internal or development environments to more robust and secure options designed for enterprise-scale production systems.

The most basic form of LDAP authentication is the anonymous bind. With an anonymous bind, the client connects to the LDAP server without providing any credentials, meaning no username or password is submitted. This type of bind results in an unauthenticated session, which typically grants limited access to public or non-sensitive directory data. For example, some organizations may configure their LDAP directory to allow anonymous reads for generic information, such as office locations or staff directories. However, anonymous access is increasingly restricted or disabled in most environments due to the security risks it presents, such as unauthorized data harvesting or exposure of organizational information to the public.

The next level of authentication is the simple bind, which is one of the most commonly used LDAP authentication methods. In a simple bind, the client submits a Distinguished Name (DN) and a password to the LDAP server. The DN identifies the specific directory entry, such as a user account, and the server verifies the provided password against the stored credential. Simple binds are straightforward to implement and supported by virtually all LDAP servers and client libraries. However, they come with a significant caveat: if the bind occurs over an unencrypted connection, the password is transmitted in clear text, exposing it to potential interception by malicious actors. To mitigate this risk, simple binds should always be performed over a secure connection, such as one protected by SSL/TLS encryption, transforming the protocol into LDAPS or utilizing StartTLS to upgrade the session.

Beyond simple binds, LDAP also supports authentication via the Simple Authentication and Security Layer, or SASL, which provides a framework for implementing more advanced and secure authentication mechanisms. SASL enables LDAP clients and servers to negotiate a range of authentication protocols based on the security requirements of the environment. Among the most common SASL mechanisms is DIGEST-MD5, which enhances security by using hashed credentials rather than transmitting passwords in clear text. With DIGEST-MD5, the client and server exchange challenge-response messages that include cryptographic hashes, providing resistance against replay and interception attacks.

Another frequently used SASL mechanism is GSSAPI, which facilitates Kerberos-based authentication. Kerberos is a network authentication protocol that provides strong mutual authentication through the use of tickets and cryptographic keys. When using GSSAPI with LDAP, clients authenticate to the LDAP server using Kerberos tickets, eliminating the need to transmit passwords entirely. This method is widely adopted in enterprise environments, particularly those that integrate LDAP with Active Directory or MIT Kerberos realms, as it supports single sign-on capabilities and enhances overall security by centralizing authentication management.

In addition to DIGEST-MD5 and GSSAPI, SASL supports mechanisms such as EXTERNAL, which leverages TLS client certificates for authentication. In environments where public key infrastructure (PKI) is implemented, LDAP clients can present digital certificates during the TLS handshake to prove their identity. This method offers a high level of security and is often used for automated systems or service accounts where password-based authentication is undesirable or insufficient. The EXTERNAL mechanism ensures that authentication occurs at the transport layer, simplifying user management and eliminating the need for passwords in the directory itself.

Many LDAP directories also integrate with external identity providers and authentication systems to facilitate centralized authentication. For example, an organization may configure its LDAP server to defer password verification to an external RADIUS server, a SAML identity provider, or an OAuth2/OpenID Connect service. In these scenarios, LDAP serves as the authoritative directory for identity data, while the actual credential verification is handled by the external service. This hybrid approach is common in modern environments where organizations seek to unify authentication across multiple services, applications, and platforms.

In operational environments, LDAP authentication methods are often chosen based on factors such as ease of integration, the sensitivity of the data, existing security infrastructure, and regulatory requirements. For example, internal applications operating within a secure network perimeter might use simple binds with TLS for convenience, while public-facing applications or services dealing with highly sensitive information may rely on Kerberos or certificate-based authentication to meet higher security standards.

LDAP also supports proxy authorization in conjunction with SASL. Proxy authorization allows a client authenticated as one identity to request operations under the authority of another user, provided that the necessary permissions are granted. This feature is useful in application-level scenarios where a service account binds to the LDAP directory and subsequently executes queries or modifications on behalf of end-users. Proxy authorization reduces the need for services to store or handle users' actual credentials, improving both security and flexibility in application design.

LDAP authentication is tightly coupled with access control, as the identity established through the bind operation dictates what the client can do within the directory. Access Control Lists, or ACLs, are applied based on the authenticated DN, limiting or granting permissions to read, write, or modify directory entries and attributes. A user authenticated through a simple bind may have rights to modify their personal entry, such as updating a telephone number or address, while an administrator authenticated via SASL GSSAPI might have elevated permissions to manage directory-wide objects like groups and policies.

Modern LDAP environments often combine multiple authentication methods to support diverse use cases. For example, service accounts used by automated scripts might authenticate using SASL EXTERNAL with client certificates, while users accessing a self-service portal might log in through a simple bind protected by TLS encryption. Administrative tools may be configured to authenticate using Kerberos tickets for seamless single sign-on, while background system integrations use stored credentials or certificate-based authentication for unattended access.

LDAP servers can also enforce authentication policies, such as password complexity rules, password expiration, and account lockout thresholds. These policies complement authentication mechanisms by ensuring that user credentials meet security best practices and reducing the risk of unauthorized access due to weak or compromised passwords. LDAP directories can enforce these policies natively or integrate with external policy enforcement points that apply organizational security standards uniformly across all authentication endpoints.

Ultimately, LDAP authentication methods form the foundation of secure directory services. From simple binds and SASL mechanisms to integration with external identity providers, each method provides varying levels of security and flexibility to meet the diverse needs of modern organizations. By selecting the appropriate authentication method and implementing strong encryption, access controls, and credential management policies, administrators can ensure that LDAP directories remain secure, reliable, and resilient against emerging threats. Understanding the strengths and limitations of each authentication method enables organizations to design directory services that balance security requirements with usability and performance.

LDAP Access Control Mechanisms

LDAP access control mechanisms are critical components of directory services that determine how users, systems, and applications interact with the data stored in the directory. By defining who can read, write, modify, or delete entries and attributes, access controls play a vital role in protecting sensitive information and enforcing organizational security policies. A well-designed access control strategy ensures that users have access to the data they need while preventing unauthorized operations that could lead to data breaches, service disruptions, or regulatory non-compliance. LDAP access control mechanisms are flexible and granular, allowing administrators to define permissions at multiple levels of the directory hierarchy.

The most common form of access control in LDAP is based on Access Control Lists, often referred to as ACLs. ACLs define rules that specify which users or groups are permitted or denied specific actions on directory entries or their attributes. These rules are evaluated by the LDAP server whenever a client attempts to perform an operation, such as reading a user's profile, updating a password, or deleting a group. ACLs can be applied to individual entries, entire subtrees, or specific attributes within an entry, providing a fine-grained approach to directory security.

A typical ACL rule includes several key elements. First, it defines the target, which could be an entire subtree, a single entry, or a specific attribute. For example, an ACL might apply to all entries under ou=HR,dc=example,dc=com or to just the mail attribute of user entries. Next, the rule defines the subjects, also known as bind DNs, that the rule applies to. Subjects can be individual users, groups, or even special categories like anonymous users or all authenticated users. Finally, the rule specifies the type of access granted or denied, such as read, write, search, compare, or manage rights.

LDAP servers process ACLs in a top-down order, evaluating each rule in sequence until a match is found or a default policy is applied. This ordering makes it essential for administrators to carefully structure their ACLs, as an overly broad rule placed higher in the list may unintentionally override more specific rules placed below. Many LDAP implementations, such as OpenLDAP, allow administrators to create multiple ACL blocks, each targeting different sections of the Directory Information Tree and addressing unique access control requirements.

For example, an ACL could be defined to allow all authenticated users to read the cn and mail attributes of other users but restrict write access to those attributes to directory administrators only. Another ACL might deny anonymous users the ability to search or read any data under the ou=Finance organizational unit, while granting members of the finance-admins group full read and write permissions within that subtree. These layered rules help enforce the principle of least privilege, ensuring users only have the minimum permissions necessary to fulfill their roles.

LDAP access controls also support attribute-level permissions, where administrators can specify different access rights for individual attributes within the same entry. This is particularly useful for user entries, where attributes like cn and mail may be publicly accessible to authenticated users, but sensitive attributes such as userPassword or employeeID are restricted to administrative accounts. Attribute-level ACLs enable organizations to protect critical data without entirely blocking access to less sensitive directory information.

Some LDAP implementations extend access control with role-based access control (RBAC) mechanisms. In an RBAC model, permissions are associated with roles, and users are assigned to those roles based on their job functions. For example, a role called HR-Manager might grant full access to employee records under ou=HR, while a role called IT-Admin might grant full control over group and device entries. RBAC simplifies access control administration by grouping permissions into logical roles, reducing the complexity of managing individual ACLs for each user.

Dynamic group membership is another feature that complements LDAP access control mechanisms. Instead of relying solely on static group definitions, dynamic groups determine their members based on LDAP search filters. This allows administrators to define groups where membership is automatically updated based on user attributes. For example, a dynamic group might include all entries where department equals Engineering. Dynamic groups can then be referenced in ACLs, providing automatic access control adjustments as users change departments or job roles without manual group management.

LDAP servers also allow for special subjects in ACLs, such as self, which represents the currently authenticated user's own entry. Using self in an ACL makes it easy to define rules that allow users to update their personal information, such as changing a phone number or home address, while restricting them from modifying data belonging to others. Another common special subject is anonymous, used to define permissions for unauthenticated connections. Many directories use anonymous rules to block read access entirely or to allow only limited access to non-sensitive public attributes.

In environments where LDAP directories are integrated with external authentication systems like Kerberos or federated identity providers, access control rules still apply within the LDAP directory itself. Even though the authentication step might be handled externally, the LDAP server uses ACLs to evaluate whether the authenticated user can perform specific operations based on their DN, group memberships, or attributes provided during the bind operation.

LDAP access controls are not limited to data operations alone. Many servers also allow administrators to define access rules that control who can perform administrative actions, such as managing schema definitions, initiating replication, or configuring directory settings. These system-level permissions are critical for maintaining the security and stability of the directory infrastructure, ensuring that only authorized personnel can modify critical server configurations or impact directory availability.

Auditing and logging are essential aspects of LDAP access control mechanisms. Directory servers typically log access attempts, both successful and denied, providing administrators with visibility into how directory data is being used and by whom. This logging is crucial for compliance with regulatory frameworks, such as GDPR or HIPAA, where organizations must demonstrate that access to personal or sensitive data is restricted and monitored. Regular audits of ACL configurations and access logs help organizations identify misconfigurations, detect potential security incidents, and enforce adherence to internal security policies.

When designing LDAP access control policies, administrators must balance security, usability, and operational efficiency. Overly permissive ACLs can expose sensitive data and create security vulnerabilities, while excessively restrictive rules may hinder legitimate users or applications from performing necessary operations. A well-designed access control strategy takes into account organizational structure, user roles, data sensitivity, and operational workflows to ensure that directory services support both security and productivity objectives.

LDAP access control mechanisms provide a powerful framework for securing directory services at multiple levels of granularity. Whether managing permissions at the entry level, the attribute level, or through dynamic groups and role-based models, administrators have the tools to implement precise and adaptable access policies. Proper use of these mechanisms is key to building a secure and compliant LDAP directory service that protects critical data while enabling smooth and efficient operations for all users and systems that depend on it.

LDIF: LDAP Data Interchange Format

The LDAP Data Interchange Format, commonly known as LDIF, is a standard plain-text format used for representing LDAP directory entries and update operations. LDIF plays a crucial role in LDAP directory administration by providing a simple, structured way to describe entries and modifications outside of the directory server itself. Administrators and automation scripts rely heavily on LDIF files for tasks such as importing large datasets into the directory, exporting directory content for backup or migration, and performing batch updates to existing entries. Because LDIF is both human-readable and machine-processable, it serves as the universal language for transferring LDAP directory data between systems.

At its most basic level, an LDIF file consists of a series of records, where each record corresponds to a single LDAP entry or a modification instruction. Each record is separated by a blank line, and within each record, attributes are expressed as key-value pairs, one per line. The most fundamental element of an LDIF record is the dn (Distinguished Name) line, which specifies the unique location of the entry within the Directory Information Tree. This is followed by one or more attribute lines that define the data contained in the entry. For example, an LDIF record for a user might begin with dn: cn=Alice Johnson,ou=Sales,dc=example,dc=com and continue with attributes such as cn: Alice Johnson, sn: Johnson, and mail: alice.johnson@example.com.

LDIF files are commonly used to create new entries within the directory using LDAP tools such as ldapadd. The LDIF file describes the new entry, including its object classes and all required attributes. Object classes are declared using the objectClass attribute and determine the type of entry being created, whether it be a user, a group, or an organizational unit. For instance, to create a user entry, the objectClass might include inetOrgPerson and organizationalPerson. When the LDIF file is processed by the ldapadd command, the LDAP server checks the schema to ensure that all required attributes for the specified object classes are present and properly formatted before accepting the new entry into the directory.

LDIF is also used for exporting directory content. The ldapsearch utility, for example, can output query results in LDIF format. This is helpful for backing up parts of the directory or preparing data for migration to another server. When exporting entries to an LDIF file, all attributes of the entries, including the dn and objectClass, are captured, preserving the complete structure and content of the directory objects. These exported files can later be imported into another LDAP server using ldapadd, ensuring that directory structures and data are replicated accurately.

In addition to describing entries, LDIF supports modification instructions through the changetype keyword. The changetype directive specifies the type of operation to be performed, such as add, modify, delete, or modrdn (modify RDN). For example, a changetype: modify record includes a series of operations like add, delete, or replace that target specific attributes within the existing entry. Each operation is followed by the attribute to be changed and its corresponding values. This allows administrators to perform complex updates in a single LDIF file, applying multiple attribute changes in a structured, batch format.

The add changetype is used when creating new entries in the directory, and in practice, an LDIF record with changetype: add is similar to a basic entry creation record, listing the dn, object classes, and attributes. The delete changetype is used to remove an entry from the directory, requiring only the dn and changetype: delete lines. The replace changetype within a modify block is used to update the value of an existing attribute, such as changing a user's job title or department. The delete operation within a modify block allows for the removal of specific attribute values or entire attributes, depending on whether a value is specified.

LDIF also supports the modrdn operation, which allows entries to be renamed or moved within the directory tree. The changetype: modrdn directive specifies the new RDN for the entry, and optional lines can indicate whether to delete the old RDN and whether to specify a new parent DN. This is commonly used in directory reorganization projects, where users or departments need to be moved to different parts of the hierarchy.

One of the advantages of LDIF is its ability to handle multi-valued attributes efficiently. For attributes that can accept multiple values, such as member in group entries or mail in user entries, LDIF allows each value to be specified on a separate line using the same attribute key. This format is intuitive and allows for easy reading and modification of data files. For example, a group entry might include multiple member: lines, each pointing to a different user's DN.

LDIF also accommodates non-ASCII or binary data by using base64 encoding. When an attribute value contains special or non-printable characters, it is encoded in base64, and the attribute line is marked with a double colon (::) after the attribute name. This ensures that directory data such as JPEG photos or complex Unicode strings can be safely represented and transferred using LDIF.

When working with LDIF, administrators must be mindful of line wrapping rules. According to the LDIF specification, any line that exceeds 76 characters should be folded onto the next line with a single space at the beginning of the continuation line. This folding helps ensure compatibility with a wide range of LDAP tools and parsers that process LDIF files. Although many modern tools automatically handle line wrapping and unfolding, understanding this convention is important when manually editing LDIF files.

LDIF files are frequently used as part of automation and provisioning workflows. For example, during mass onboarding of new employees, an HR system might generate an LDIF file containing all user entries to be created, which is then processed by ldapadd to bulk-insert the new accounts into the directory. Similarly, cleanup scripts might generate LDIF files with changetype: delete directives to remove deactivated accounts or obsolete resources from the directory.

Another common use case is schema extension. Administrators can define custom schema elements in LDIF format, specifying new object classes, attribute types, and matching rules. These schema definitions are then imported into the directory using ldapadd or the LDAP server's configuration utilities. By managing schema changes in LDIF format, organizations maintain clear documentation of schema extensions and ensure that modifications can be version-controlled alongside other infrastructure configurations.

LDIF provides a standardized, versatile, and efficient way to manage LDAP data outside of the directory itself. Its human-readable structure makes it accessible for administrators to create, modify, and audit directory data, while its compatibility with automated tools and scripts supports scalable operations in large and complex environments. Mastering LDIF is a key skill for any LDAP administrator, enabling them to efficiently manage directory content and streamline both routine and large-scale directory operations.

LDAP Replication Concepts

LDAP replication is a critical concept for ensuring the availability, reliability, and scalability of directory services across distributed systems. Replication involves the process of copying directory data from one LDAP server to one or more additional servers, maintaining consistent data across multiple locations. This approach provides fault tolerance, improves performance by reducing client load on a single server, and enables geographical distribution of directory services for organizations with multiple sites or data centers. LDAP replication is especially important in environments where directory data must be accessible at all times, even in the event of hardware failures, network outages, or maintenance windows.

The fundamental principle behind LDAP replication is that one LDAP server, known as the provider or master, shares its directory information with one or more replica servers, commonly referred to as consumers or slaves. The provider server is responsible for handling all write operations, such as add, delete, and modify requests, while the consumer servers receive copies of these changes and make them available for read operations. This master-slave replication model, also known as single-master replication, has been widely adopted due to its simplicity and ability to reduce contention on write operations by consolidating them on a single server.

In single-master replication, all directory modifications occur on the master server, and these changes are then propagated to the consumers using a replication protocol such as LDAP Sync Replication or custom synchronization mechanisms provided by the LDAP server implementation. For example, OpenLDAP uses the syncrepl engine to handle replication, while Microsoft Active Directory employs its own proprietary replication protocols that synchronize changes between domain controllers. The consumer servers apply the changes they receive to their local copies of the directory data, ensuring that all servers remain synchronized and consistent over time.

The advantages of single-master replication include reduced risk of data conflicts, as there is only one authoritative source for write operations, and a straightforward conflict resolution model. Consumers can be distributed across different locations or networks, allowing users and applications to connect to the nearest replica for read operations, reducing latency and improving performance. Additionally, this model simplifies schema management and policy enforcement since changes to the directory schema or access controls typically occur only on the master server.

However, single-master replication also has limitations, particularly regarding scalability and resilience. Since all write operations are handled by a single server, the master can become a bottleneck under heavy write loads or during peak usage periods. Furthermore, if the master server becomes unavailable due to hardware failure or network issues, no write operations can be performed until the master is restored. To address these concerns, many organizations implement multi-master replication, also known as peer-to-peer replication.

Multi-master replication allows two or more LDAP servers to act as both providers and consumers, accepting both read and write operations and synchronizing changes between each other. This model enhances availability and fault tolerance by ensuring that no single server is a point of failure for write operations. If one server becomes unavailable, clients can still perform both read and write operations on another server in the replication topology. Multi-master replication is common in large-scale deployments and environments where high availability is a critical requirement.

While multi-master replication improves resilience, it introduces additional complexity, particularly regarding conflict resolution. Since multiple servers can accept write operations simultaneously, conflicts may arise when the same entry is modified on two servers at nearly the same time. To resolve these conflicts, LDAP servers typically employ conflict resolution algorithms, such as last-write-wins based on timestamps or custom rules defined by administrators. These mechanisms aim to ensure that all servers eventually converge on a consistent state, but administrators must be mindful of the potential for data inconsistencies if replication conflicts are not properly managed.

LDAP replication can be configured in several topologies, depending on the needs of the organization. The simplest topology is a star configuration, where one master server replicates to multiple consumer servers. This model is easy to deploy and manage but lacks redundancy for write operations. A ring topology, where each server replicates to its neighboring servers, provides more fault tolerance but requires careful planning to avoid replication loops and excessive network traffic. In complex environments, hybrid topologies combining elements of star and ring configurations may be implemented to balance redundancy, performance, and administrative simplicity.

Another important aspect of LDAP replication is the replication scope, which defines the portion of the directory tree that is replicated between servers. In some cases, organizations may choose to replicate the entire directory tree to all servers, ensuring that every replica contains a full copy of the directory. In other scenarios, partial replication may be implemented, where only specific branches or subtrees are replicated to certain servers. Partial replication is useful for limiting data exposure in environments with strict security or privacy requirements, as well as for optimizing performance by reducing the size of replicated datasets.

Replication schedules and triggers are additional considerations when designing an LDAP replication strategy. Some LDAP servers support continuous or real-time replication, where changes are propagated immediately as they occur. This approach minimizes the delay between updates on the master and their availability on consumers but may result in higher network usage. Alternatively, periodic replication can be configured to run at defined intervals, reducing network overhead but introducing a lag between updates and their propagation to other servers. The appropriate replication schedule depends on the organization's priorities for data freshness, network utilization, and system load.

LDAP replication is also crucial for disaster recovery planning. By maintaining replica servers in geographically separate data centers, organizations can protect against data loss or service interruptions caused by regional outages. If one site becomes unavailable, users and applications can failover to a remote replica, ensuring business continuity. To further enhance disaster recovery capabilities, some LDAP environments incorporate backup and restore mechanisms alongside replication, allowing for point-in-time recovery in the event of catastrophic failures or data corruption.

In modern cloud and hybrid deployments, LDAP replication extends beyond on-premises servers. Many organizations now replicate directory data between on-premises LDAP servers and cloud-based directory services, such as cloud LDAP or identity-as-a-service platforms. This hybrid approach allows organizations to provide a unified directory experience for users across both on-premises and cloud applications, while maintaining control over sensitive identity data and adhering to regulatory requirements.

LDAP replication concepts are foundational to building a resilient, scalable, and highly available directory infrastructure. Whether deploying a simple single-master replication model or a complex multi-master configuration spanning multiple regions, understanding the principles of replication enables administrators to design and maintain directory services that meet the operational, performance, and security needs of their organizations. By carefully planning replication topologies, conflict resolution strategies, and replication scopes, administrators can ensure that their LDAP environments remain robust, consistent, and capable of supporting critical identity and access management functions across diverse IT landscapes.

Multi-Master vs. Single-Master Replication

In LDAP directory services, replication is essential for ensuring high availability, scalability, and data redundancy across distributed environments. Two primary models dominate the replication landscape: single-master replication and multi-master replication. Each model provides distinct benefits and trade-offs, and choosing the right approach is a key architectural decision that impacts the performance, reliability, and complexity of the directory system. Both models aim to ensure that directory data remains consistent across multiple LDAP servers, but they differ significantly in how write operations are handled and how data synchronization occurs.

Single-master replication, sometimes called master-slave replication, involves one authoritative server, referred to as the master or provider, which handles all write operations. This server is responsible for processing all changes, including additions, deletions, and modifications to directory entries. The master then replicates these changes to one or more read-only consumer servers, also known as slaves. Consumers receive updates from the master server at regular intervals or through real-time replication mechanisms, depending on the configuration. While consumers can respond to read queries, they cannot process write operations directly. Any client attempting to make a change on a consumer server is typically redirected to the master.

The single-master model has several advantages, starting with its simplicity. Having a single authoritative source for write operations minimizes the risk of data conflicts because all changes flow through a single server. This simplicity makes it easier to enforce schema consistency, data validation rules, and business logic since the master controls all updates. Additionally, single-master replication allows for more predictable and straightforward troubleshooting and auditing. Any unexpected changes or anomalies can typically be traced back to the master, where all write operations originate. Administrators also benefit from having a centralized point of control, which simplifies processes like access control configuration and schema updates.

Single-master replication, however, comes with limitations. The most significant challenge is the potential for the master server to become a bottleneck under heavy write loads, especially in large or globally distributed environments. All write traffic must be directed to the master, which can create performance and scalability constraints. If the master becomes unavailable due to hardware failure, network outage, or maintenance, write operations are temporarily halted until the master is restored. While read operations on consumer servers remain functional, the inability to process writes can disrupt workflows that depend on real-time data updates, such as user provisioning, group membership changes, or dynamic access control adjustments.

To address these limitations, multi-master replication introduces a more distributed approach. In multi-master replication, two or more LDAP servers act as peers, each capable of handling both read and write operations. Changes made to any server in the replication topology are automatically propagated to all other servers, ensuring that data remains synchronized across the environment. This model eliminates the single point of failure for write operations, enhancing system resilience and supporting high-availability requirements. If one server goes offline, clients can still perform both read and write operations on other servers in the topology, reducing downtime and improving the user experience.

Multi-master replication also provides performance benefits by distributing the write load across multiple servers. In large organizations with geographically dispersed offices, users and applications can connect to the nearest server for both reads and writes, reducing latency and optimizing network efficiency. This is particularly valuable in environments where local offices or data centers need to perform frequent updates to directory data while maintaining real-time synchronization with the wider organization.

Despite its advantages, multi-master replication introduces additional complexity, particularly around conflict resolution. Since multiple servers can accept write operations simultaneously, it is possible for two servers to receive conflicting updates to the same entry or attribute. For example, if two administrators in different regions modify the same user's phone number on different servers at nearly the same time, a conflict arises. To resolve these situations, LDAP servers implementing multi-master replication typically rely on conflict resolution mechanisms, such as timestamp-based logic or custom rules. A common approach is last-write-wins, where the update with the most recent timestamp takes precedence. However, this method can result in unintended overwrites if administrators are unaware of concurrent changes.

The increased complexity of multi-master replication extends to deployment and maintenance. Administrators must carefully design the replication topology to avoid excessive replication traffic and ensure timely synchronization. Circular replication loops, excessive replication latency, and inconsistent access control policies can all lead to data integrity issues if not properly managed. Additionally, schema changes in multi-master environments require coordinated deployment across all servers to prevent schema mismatches and replication errors.

Security considerations also differ between the two models. In single-master replication, administrators can enforce stricter access controls by limiting write permissions to the master server, reducing the attack surface for unauthorized data modifications. In multi-master replication, every participating server must be secured to prevent unauthorized writes from occurring on any node in the topology. This necessitates more rigorous auditing, access control policies, and monitoring to ensure that all servers uphold the organization's security posture.

When deciding between single-master and multi-master replication, organizations must evaluate their operational needs, network architecture, and business continuity requirements. Single-master replication is often sufficient for small to mid-sized organizations where the directory serves a single data center or where write operations are relatively infrequent and predictable. It provides a stable, easy-to-manage environment with fewer moving parts and simpler administrative procedures.

On the other hand, multi-master replication is the preferred choice for enterprises with high availability demands, global footprints, or mission-critical applications that require continuous write access across multiple sites. It offers better fault tolerance and scalability but requires a higher level of administrative expertise to configure and maintain effectively.

Some organizations implement hybrid approaches that combine the strengths of both models. For example, a multi-master topology might be deployed across regional hubs, while each hub uses single-master replication to distribute data to read-only consumer servers at branch offices. This layered approach provides a balance between high availability, reduced latency, and simplified administration in remote locations.

Ultimately, both single-master and multi-master replication models are essential tools in the LDAP administrator's toolkit. Each model serves specific purposes and fits particular organizational structures and workloads. A thorough understanding of their benefits, limitations, and trade-offs allows organizations to design directory infrastructures that align with their technical requirements and business goals. Careful planning, combined with proactive monitoring and maintenance, ensures that LDAP replication—regardless of the chosen model—delivers the expected performance, reliability, and consistency required for modern identity and access management environments.

LDAP Synchronization Strategies

LDAP synchronization strategies are essential for ensuring consistency between multiple LDAP servers and between LDAP directories and external systems. In any organization that depends on a directory service to manage users, groups, devices, and resources, keeping directory data synchronized is critical for maintaining data integrity, enabling seamless authentication, and supporting accurate authorization processes. Synchronization strategies are particularly important in distributed environments where multiple replicas of the directory may exist across geographically dispersed locations or when integrating LDAP directories with external identity providers, HR systems, or cloud-based applications.

One of the most common synchronization strategies in LDAP is replication-based synchronization. In this approach, changes made on one LDAP server are automatically propagated to one or more other LDAP servers. This can occur in real-time, where changes are pushed to replicas immediately as they occur, or on a scheduled basis, where updates are transmitted at defined intervals. Replication-based synchronization is typically handled by the LDAP server itself, using built-in mechanisms such as OpenLDAP's syncrepl or Microsoft Active Directory's native replication protocols. These mechanisms are highly efficient for maintaining synchronization within the same directory infrastructure, such as between master and consumer servers in single-master replication or between peer servers in multi-master configurations.

Replication-based synchronization can be configured for full or partial directory trees. Full tree synchronization replicates all entries and attributes from the source to the target server, ensuring an identical copy of the directory data. This approach is often used when providing high availability across data centers or when deploying redundant servers for disaster recovery. Partial synchronization, on the other hand, replicates only specific branches of the Directory Information Tree or selected attributes. This can be useful when limiting data exposure to certain regions or departments or when reducing network and storage overhead by replicating only essential data.

Another widely used strategy is scheduled batch synchronization. In this method, synchronization jobs are executed at regular intervals, such as every hour, daily, or weekly. These jobs typically involve exporting directory data to LDIF or CSV files and then importing them into the target system. Scheduled batch synchronization is commonly used when integrating LDAP with external databases, HR systems, or identity management platforms that do not support real-time integration. Although this strategy introduces some delay between updates and synchronization, it is suitable for environments where real-time consistency is not critical. Additionally, batch synchronization is easier to troubleshoot and monitor, as administrators can review logs and reports after each job completes.

A key consideration when designing LDAP synchronization strategies is change detection. To avoid synchronizing the entire directory every time, most synchronization tools implement change detection mechanisms that identify only the entries or attributes that have been modified since the last synchronization cycle. LDAP servers often include attributes such as modifyTimestamp or entryCSN (Change Sequence Number), which record the last modification time or a unique change identifier for each entry. Synchronization tools can query these attributes to build incremental change sets, reducing the amount of data transferred and improving synchronization efficiency.

For more advanced scenarios, directory synchronization gateways or middleware platforms are used to synchronize LDAP directories with external services such as Microsoft Azure AD, Google Workspace, or cloud-based SaaS applications. These tools, often referred to as identity synchronization or meta-directory solutions, act as intermediaries that map directory schemas, transform data formats, and handle protocol differences between systems. For example, a meta-directory might synchronize LDAP user accounts with Azure AD by converting LDAP attributes to match Azure's schema requirements and transmitting changes via RESTful APIs or SCIM (System for Cross-domain Identity Management) protocols.

Real-time synchronization through event-driven mechanisms is another approach gaining traction in modern environments. In event-driven synchronization, LDAP servers or synchronization tools listen for directory events, such as the creation of a new user or the modification of a group membership, and immediately trigger synchronization processes. Technologies like LDAP persistent search or the LDAP Content Synchronization (RFC 4533) standard enable clients to receive change notifications as they happen, allowing for near-instantaneous updates to external systems. Event-driven synchronization is ideal for use cases where timely updates are crucial, such as when synchronizing authentication data with cloud applications or when enforcing compliance and audit requirements that demand up-to-date directory records.

LDAP synchronization strategies must also account for conflict resolution. When synchronizing data between multiple systems, discrepancies may arise due to concurrent updates, schema mismatches, or differing business rules. Conflict resolution mechanisms typically rely on rules such as last-write-wins, where the most recent change takes precedence, or on priority-based models, where one system is designated as authoritative for specific attributes. Some synchronization platforms offer advanced conflict resolution capabilities, allowing administrators to define custom logic based on data values, source systems, or timestamps to handle conflicts more intelligently.

Security is a critical aspect of LDAP synchronization. Synchronization processes often involve the transmission of sensitive identity data, including user credentials, contact details, and access rights. To protect this information, synchronization channels should always be encrypted using SSL/TLS or other secure transport protocols. Additionally, synchronization tools and services must authenticate securely with both the LDAP directory and external systems, adhering to the principle of least privilege by using service accounts with only the necessary permissions to read or modify data.

Another consideration is data transformation and attribute mapping. Different systems may use varying attribute names, data formats, or structural models for representing identity information. For example, an LDAP directory might use the attribute uid to store usernames, while an external system may require sAMAccountName or userPrincipalName. Synchronization tools must perform data transformations to reconcile these differences, ensuring that synchronized records are accurate and usable in the target system. This often involves writing transformation rules or scripts that manipulate data before it is imported into or exported from the LDAP directory.

Error handling and monitoring are also vital for successful LDAP synchronization. Synchronization processes must include mechanisms for detecting and handling failures, such as missing required attributes, schema violations, or network connectivity issues. Automated retry mechanisms, alerting systems, and detailed logging help administrators identify and resolve issues quickly, ensuring that directory synchronization remains reliable and consistent. Monitoring tools can also provide insights into synchronization performance, including metrics such as processing time, the number of entries synchronized, and the volume of data transferred.

In large organizations, synchronization strategies may involve multiple stages or tiers. For example, a central LDAP directory might synchronize with regional directories in different countries, which in turn synchronize with local applications and services. This hierarchical approach helps distribute load, minimize latency, and localize directory data while ensuring that critical identity information is synchronized organization-wide.

LDAP synchronization strategies play a pivotal role in maintaining the coherence and availability of directory data in distributed environments. Whether through replication, batch jobs, real-time event processing, or meta-directory platforms, synchronization ensures that users, applications, and systems have timely and accurate access to identity data. By implementing robust synchronization strategies, organizations can achieve seamless interoperability between LDAP directories and external systems, enhance the resilience of their identity infrastructure, and meet the performance and security demands of modern IT environments.

Integrating LDAP with Applications

Integrating LDAP with applications is a critical aspect of building centralized identity and access management solutions in modern IT environments. LDAP serves as a central directory that holds user identities, group memberships, and other resource-related information, making it an ideal backend for applications that require user authentication, authorization, and user data retrieval. By leveraging LDAP as a single source of truth, organizations can simplify user management, enhance security, and ensure consistency across multiple systems and services. The process of integrating applications with LDAP varies depending on the application's architecture, the programming languages used, and the directory schema, but the fundamental principles are widely applicable.

One of the most common use cases for LDAP integration is user authentication. Many applications, such as web portals, intranets, content management systems, and enterprise applications, require users to log in before accessing protected resources. Instead of managing separate user databases within each application, administrators can configure applications to delegate authentication to an LDAP directory. In this setup, when a user attempts to log in, the application performs an LDAP bind operation using the user's Distinguished Name and password. If the bind is successful, the user is authenticated, and access to the application is granted according to the application's authorization rules.

To facilitate this process, applications typically perform an LDAP search operation to locate the user's entry in the directory based on a unique identifier, such as uid, cn, or mail. Once the application retrieves the user's DN, it can perform the bind operation. This search-and-bind workflow ensures that user authentication leverages the centralized credentials stored in the LDAP directory, eliminating the need to manage local user accounts within the application itself. Most modern applications, frameworks, and middleware platforms provide built-in modules, libraries, or plugins to simplify LDAP authentication integration.

Beyond authentication, LDAP integration also enables applications to perform authorization based on group memberships or user attributes stored in the directory. For example, an application might query LDAP to determine if a user is a member of a specific group, such as cn=admins,ou=groups,dc=example,dc=com, before granting access to administrative functions. This approach is known as role-based access control (RBAC), where LDAP groups define user roles, and applications enforce permissions based on group memberships. By centralizing authorization data in LDAP, administrators can manage access rights consistently across multiple applications, reducing the risk of privilege creep and security misconfigurations.

Many web applications and platforms also integrate LDAP for user provisioning and profile synchronization. Instead of manually entering user details during account creation, applications can query LDAP for attributes such as givenName, sn, mail, department, and title, automatically populating user profiles based on directory data. This reduces administrative overhead and ensures that user profiles within applications reflect accurate and up-to-date information. In environments where applications support self-service profile updates, integration can also be configured to push changes back to the LDAP directory, ensuring bi-directional synchronization.

Single sign-on (SSO) systems often rely on LDAP directories as their underlying identity providers. In an SSO environment, users authenticate once to the SSO platform, which then issues tokens or assertions to integrated applications, allowing seamless access without re-entering credentials. LDAP serves as the authentication backend for the SSO system, which might use protocols such as SAML, OAuth2, or OpenID Connect to federate identities across web applications, cloud services, and legacy systems. Integrating LDAP with SSO platforms enhances user convenience and improves security by reducing password fatigue and consolidating authentication points.

Another important aspect of LDAP integration is directory searches for user discovery and organizational data lookups. Applications like internal directories, collaboration tools, and email clients often need to display user contact information or organizational charts. By integrating with LDAP, these applications can perform LDAP search queries to retrieve directory entries based on filters like (department=Marketing) or (title=Manager). The search results can then be used to build dynamic user directories, facilitate team collaboration, or populate mailing lists based on LDAP groups.

From a development perspective, integrating LDAP with custom applications typically involves using LDAP client libraries provided for various programming languages. For example, the python-ldap library allows Python developers to perform LDAP operations such as search, bind, and modify directly within their applications. Java developers can use the JNDI API to integrate LDAP queries into Java EE applications, while PHP applications often use libraries like phpLDAP or native LDAP functions to connect to LDAP servers. These libraries abstract much of the complexity of LDAP communication and provide high-level methods for interacting with directory data.

Security is a key consideration when integrating LDAP with applications. Applications should always use secure LDAP (LDAPS) or

StartTLS to encrypt communications with the directory server, protecting credentials and directory data from interception. Additionally, applications should be configured to perform LDAP bind operations using service accounts with minimal privileges necessary for the task at hand. For example, an application that only needs to perform read operations should not use a service account with write access to the directory.

Performance optimization is also critical, especially in large environments with thousands of directory entries. Applications should use well-designed LDAP search filters and limit the scope of queries to specific organizational units or subtrees whenever possible. Indexing frequently queried attributes, such as uid, cn, or mail, on the LDAP server further improves query performance and reduces server load. In some cases, applications may implement caching mechanisms to store frequently accessed directory data locally, reducing the frequency of LDAP queries and improving response times.

Integrating LDAP with applications also introduces considerations related to schema alignment. Applications often expect specific attributes to be present in the directory, such as givenName or displayName, which may not exist in all LDAP schemas. Administrators may need to extend the LDAP schema to include missing attributes or configure attribute mappings within the application to ensure compatibility. Clear documentation of schema requirements and attribute usage is essential to avoid integration challenges.

Audit and compliance requirements often mandate that LDAP-integrated applications log authentication attempts and access control decisions. Integrating with LDAP allows applications to offload some of these responsibilities to the directory service, which typically logs all bind operations and directory access events. However, applications should still maintain internal logs that capture user actions within the application itself, providing a comprehensive audit trail.

LDAP integration extends beyond traditional web applications and includes network services, such as VPN gateways, Wi-Fi authentication portals, and Unix/Linux PAM (Pluggable Authentication Module) systems. These services can authenticate users against LDAP directories, providing centralized authentication across infrastructure components. For example, configuring a Linux server to authenticate users via LDAP allows employees to log in with their directory credentials, streamlining account management and ensuring consistent access policies across systems.

Integrating LDAP with applications creates a unified identity management ecosystem that simplifies administration, enhances security, and improves the user experience. By centralizing authentication, authorization, and user data retrieval in LDAP, organizations can reduce operational complexity, enforce consistent security policies, and support scalable growth across on-premises and cloud environments. Whether through simple authentication workflows or complex SSO federations, LDAP remains a foundational technology for building secure and efficient enterprise applications.

LDAP and Single Sign-On (SSO)

LDAP and Single Sign-On (SSO) are two technologies that, when integrated, provide organizations with a seamless and secure authentication experience across multiple applications and services. LDAP serves as a centralized directory service that stores user credentials and identity information, while SSO allows users to authenticate once and gain access to multiple systems without being prompted to re-enter their credentials. Together, LDAP and SSO reduce administrative overhead, enhance user productivity, and strengthen security by consolidating authentication workflows into a unified infrastructure.

At the core of LDAP's value in an SSO environment is its role as the authoritative identity provider. LDAP directories, such as OpenLDAP, Microsoft Active Directory, or Red Hat Directory Server, maintain user accounts, group memberships, roles, and various attributes necessary for identity management. When SSO platforms are deployed, they often rely on LDAP directories as the backend source for authenticating users and retrieving identity attributes. During the initial authentication process, the SSO system interacts with the LDAP server to validate user credentials through a bind operation. Once the user is authenticated, the SSO platform issues a security token or assertion that the user can present to integrated applications and services, granting them access without requiring further logins.

A typical SSO workflow begins with the user navigating to an application that is protected by SSO. If the user does not yet have an active SSO session, they are redirected to the SSO login portal. Here, the user provides their LDAP-based credentials, such as a username and password, which the SSO platform verifies by performing an LDAP bind against the directory server. If the credentials are valid, the SSO system creates a session and issues a token, such as a SAML assertion, OAuth2 token, or OpenID Connect ID token. This token serves as proof of authentication and is presented to other applications that participate in the SSO ecosystem.

One of the most common SSO protocols used alongside LDAP is SAML (Security Assertion Markup Language). SAML enables secure exchange of authentication and authorization data between an identity provider (IdP) and service providers (SPs). In this setup, the SSO platform acts as the IdP, authenticating users against LDAP and issuing SAML assertions to SPs when users attempt to access protected applications. The SAML assertion contains information about the authenticated user, such as their username, email address, and group memberships, allowing the application to grant access based on predefined policies. Because the SAML assertion is digitally signed by the IdP, service providers can trust the validity of the authentication without directly interacting with LDAP.

LDAP and SSO also work together in OAuth2 and OpenID Connect (OIDC) implementations. In this model, LDAP serves as the identity source for the authorization server, which is part of the OAuth2 or OIDC framework. When a user initiates an authentication request, the authorization server queries the LDAP directory to validate the user's credentials and retrieve user attributes. Upon successful authentication, the authorization server issues access tokens and ID tokens that are consumed by applications and APIs to establish user sessions. This approach is common in modern web and mobile application architectures where APIs and microservices require secure, token-based authentication mechanisms.

The integration of LDAP with SSO reduces the number of times users need to authenticate as they move between applications. This improves user experience by eliminating the frustration of multiple login prompts, which is particularly valuable in enterprise environments where employees may access dozens of systems daily. The streamlined login process not only increases productivity but also reduces the risk of password fatigue, where users resort to insecure practices such as reusing weak passwords across systems.

From a security perspective, combining LDAP with SSO enables centralized control over authentication policies. Password complexity rules, account lockout thresholds, and multi-factor authentication (MFA) requirements can be enforced at the LDAP level and extended to all SSO-enabled applications. Additionally, SSO platforms often support integrations with identity governance tools that allow organizations to define role-based access controls, automate user provisioning and deprovisioning, and audit authentication events across all connected services. This centralized approach improves regulatory compliance and provides greater visibility into user activity.

Another advantage of integrating LDAP with SSO is the simplification of account management. User identities and credentials are managed exclusively in LDAP, reducing the need to maintain multiple user databases across different applications. When a user is created or updated in LDAP, these changes are immediately reflected across all SSO-connected services. Likewise, when a user leaves the organization, disabling or deleting their LDAP account instantly revokes access to all integrated applications, reducing the risk of orphaned accounts and unauthorized access.

LDAP and SSO integration also supports federated identity models where multiple organizations or domains share authentication responsibilities. In such scenarios, LDAP directories from different entities can be federated through the SSO platform, allowing users from one organization to access applications in another without managing separate accounts. Federated SSO is common in partnerships, supply chains, and multi-tenant environments where users from various organizations need controlled access to shared resources.

Despite the benefits, integrating LDAP with SSO requires careful planning and configuration. Administrators must ensure that the LDAP directory is properly structured and contains all necessary attributes required by the SSO platform and connected applications. Attributes such as uid, cn, mail, and memberOf are commonly used by SSO systems to uniquely identify users and assign roles or permissions within applications. Schema extensions or attribute mapping may be necessary if certain required fields are not present in the default LDAP schema.

Security considerations include encrypting all LDAP traffic between the SSO platform and the directory server using LDAPS or StartTLS. The LDAP service account used by the SSO platform should have read-only access to user data and should be tightly scoped to the organizational units relevant to authentication. Additionally, integrating MFA solutions with SSO platforms further enhances security by requiring users to present a second factor, such as a hardware token, biometric verification, or mobile push notification, during the initial login process.

Performance optimization is another factor to consider when integrating LDAP with SSO. Authentication requests from the SSO platform should be directed to LDAP servers that are geographically close to reduce latency, particularly in global organizations. Deploying replica LDAP servers or using a global load balancer to distribute authentication traffic can improve responsiveness and fault tolerance. Some SSO solutions also implement caching mechanisms that store recently retrieved directory attributes, reducing the frequency of LDAP queries and improving performance.

LDAP and Single Sign-On create a powerful combination for building secure, user-friendly, and scalable authentication architectures. By centralizing identity management within LDAP and leveraging SSO protocols to federate authentication across multiple applications and services, organizations can reduce administrative complexity, enhance security posture, and deliver a superior experience to users. This integration is a cornerstone of modern identity and access management frameworks, supporting the needs of enterprises as they navigate increasingly complex and distributed IT landscapes.

LDAP and Identity Management

LDAP and identity management are closely intertwined, as LDAP serves as one of the foundational technologies for managing digital identities within an organization. Identity management refers to the processes and systems used to create, maintain, and govern user identities, as well as to control access to resources based on those identities. LDAP provides the directory service component that acts as a centralized repository for storing identity information, such as usernames, passwords, email addresses, group memberships, and other critical attributes. This centralized model plays a key role in enabling secure access to applications, services, and systems throughout the organization.

LDAP directories form the backbone of identity management infrastructures by providing a structured, hierarchical, and easily searchable database of user accounts and related objects. Every identity stored in LDAP is represented as an entry, which is uniquely identified by a distinguished name and structured according to object classes defined in the directory schema. User entries often use object classes like inetOrgPerson or organizationalPerson, which define the set of attributes used to represent a user. These attributes typically include essential information such as the common name, surname, email address, department, and user ID. In addition to user entries, LDAP directories also store groups, organizational units, devices, and roles, which together facilitate the implementation of access controls and policy enforcement.

One of the most important functions of LDAP within identity management is authentication. By centralizing user credentials in a single directory, LDAP enables multiple systems and applications to validate users' identities without maintaining redundant databases. When a user attempts to access a system or service, the system queries the LDAP directory to verify the user's credentials. This is typically achieved through a bind operation, where the user provides a username and password, and LDAP validates them against the stored values. By serving as the authoritative source for user authentication,

LDAP helps enforce consistent security policies and reduces the complexity of managing credentials across a distributed environment.

LDAP also plays a critical role in authorization by providing the necessary data to determine what actions a user is permitted to perform. Many identity management solutions use LDAP groups and roles to implement role-based access control (RBAC). In this model, users are assigned to groups within LDAP, such as cn=finance or cn=engineering, and applications reference these groups when determining whether to grant or deny access to specific resources. This centralized approach to managing permissions simplifies administrative tasks, as group membership changes in LDAP are immediately reflected across all integrated applications.

Provisioning and deprovisioning are additional core components of identity management that are facilitated by LDAP. When a new employee joins an organization, their identity is created in the LDAP directory, typically as part of an onboarding process integrated with human resources systems. This new LDAP entry is then used to automatically provision access to required applications, network services, and resources. Conversely, when an employee leaves the organization, their LDAP account can be disabled or removed, instantly revoking access to all connected systems and reducing the risk of security breaches caused by orphaned accounts.

LDAP directories also support delegated administration, a key feature in identity management for large organizations with complex hierarchies. Delegated administration allows different administrative teams to manage specific sections of the directory tree. For example, the IT team responsible for the engineering department might be granted permissions to manage user accounts within ou=engineering,dc=example,dc=com, while HR administrators manage user accounts under ou=hr. This delegation model streamlines administrative workflows while maintaining centralized control over directory structure and security policies.

Identity synchronization is another area where LDAP contributes significantly to identity management. Many organizations operate multiple directories or need to synchronize LDAP with other identity stores, such as cloud identity providers, HR systems, or customer databases. LDAP synchronization ensures that identity data remains consistent across systems, enabling seamless access to resources regardless of where authentication takes place. Tools and protocols such as LDAP Content Synchronization (RFC 4533), meta-directories, and identity bridges facilitate synchronization, reducing data duplication and minimizing administrative overhead.

Modern identity management also leverages LDAP for supporting federation and single sign-on (SSO) capabilities. LDAP often serves as the backend for identity providers (IdPs) that participate in SSO ecosystems using protocols like SAML, OAuth2, or OpenID Connect. In these architectures, LDAP provides the authoritative user store, while the IdP handles token issuance and federation to external service providers. This integration allows users to authenticate once to the IdP using their LDAP credentials and gain access to multiple applications without re-authenticating, streamlining the user experience and improving security by reducing reliance on multiple sets of credentials.

Security enforcement is another major aspect of LDAP-based identity management. LDAP directories help enforce password policies, such as complexity requirements, expiration periods, and lockout mechanisms after repeated failed login attempts. Additionally, LDAP supports integration with multi-factor authentication (MFA) systems that require users to provide additional verification factors, such as hardware tokens or mobile push notifications, in conjunction with their LDAP credentials. By implementing centralized security policies through LDAP, organizations can maintain a strong security posture while simplifying compliance with industry regulations and standards.

Audit and compliance reporting is further enhanced by LDAP's role in identity management. LDAP servers maintain logs of access and authentication attempts, including details such as timestamps, source IP addresses, and the outcome of bind operations. These logs are critical for auditing user activity, detecting anomalies, and investigating security incidents. Combined with identity governance tools, LDAP-based identity management frameworks enable organizations to track who has access to what resources, when changes were made, and whether access policies are being followed consistently.

LDAP's extensibility also supports diverse identity management scenarios. Administrators can extend the directory schema to introduce custom attributes and object classes tailored to the organization's specific business requirements. For example, custom attributes like employeeStatus, contractEndDate, or departmentCode can be used to enrich user profiles and drive automation workflows, such as automatically disabling accounts for contractors whose assignments have ended.

In hybrid IT environments, where organizations use both on-premises and cloud-based services, LDAP serves as the foundation for hybrid identity management strategies. LDAP directories can synchronize with cloud identity providers, enabling seamless access to Software-as-a-Service (SaaS) applications while maintaining centralized control over user data. This hybrid approach ensures that users can leverage the same LDAP identity for both internal systems and external services, enhancing operational efficiency and reducing identity sprawl.

LDAP and identity management are inseparable in modern enterprise architectures. By acting as the single source of truth for identity data, LDAP simplifies the process of managing users, groups, and resources across a wide variety of platforms. Its compatibility with standard protocols, integration with identity governance solutions, and support for centralized security policies make it a cornerstone of any robust identity management system. As organizations continue to face evolving challenges related to user access, compliance, and security, LDAP remains a critical component in building scalable and effective identity management infrastructures.

LDAP Security Best Practices

Securing an LDAP directory is paramount to protecting an organization's critical identity and access data. LDAP servers often serve as the central repository for user credentials, group memberships, access control policies, and other sensitive information that underpins authentication and authorization processes across the IT infrastructure. Because LDAP directories are a frequent target for attackers, implementing comprehensive security best practices is essential to ensure data confidentiality, integrity, and availability. A well-secured LDAP environment minimizes the risk of unauthorized access, data breaches, and service disruptions.

The first and most fundamental best practice is to always encrypt LDAP traffic. By default, LDAP operates over port 389 and transmits data, including credentials, in plain text. To prevent eavesdropping and man-in-the-middle attacks, organizations must enforce encryption by using LDAP over SSL (LDAPS) on port 636 or StartTLS to upgrade an unencrypted connection to a secure one. This ensures that all data exchanged between clients and the directory server is encrypted in transit. SSL/TLS certificates should be issued by a trusted certificate authority (CA) and regularly reviewed for expiration or revocation to avoid service interruptions and maintain trust.

Access control is another critical component of LDAP security. Directory administrators must define and enforce granular Access Control Lists (ACLs) that specify which users or services can access specific parts of the directory tree and which operations they are permitted to perform. ACLs should follow the principle of least privilege, granting users and applications only the minimum permissions necessary for their roles. For example, an application requiring read-only access to user profile data should not be granted permissions to modify entries or access sensitive attributes such as user passwords. Special attention should be given to highly sensitive entries, such as those containing administrative accounts or security-related data, by restricting access to only trusted personnel.

Service accounts used by applications to connect to the LDAP directory should be tightly controlled and isolated. Each service or application should have a unique service account with tailored permissions relevant to its function. These accounts should never share administrative privileges unless absolutely necessary. Furthermore, service accounts should be subject to password policies, including password complexity requirements, expiration periods, and regular password rotation, to reduce the likelihood of compromise.

Disabling or severely limiting anonymous binds is an essential LDAP security measure. Anonymous binds allow clients to connect to the directory without authentication, which could expose sensitive directory information to unauthorized parties. Unless there is a specific business requirement, such as allowing limited read access to public data, anonymous access should be disabled to ensure that all clients must authenticate before interacting with the directory.

Regularly auditing and monitoring LDAP activity is crucial for detecting unauthorized access attempts, unusual behavior, and potential security incidents. LDAP servers generate logs of all authentication requests, directory modifications, and access attempts, including the DN used, IP address, timestamp, and operation outcome. These logs should be reviewed regularly and integrated with a centralized security information and event management (SIEM) system to enable real-time alerting and correlation with other security events across the environment. Proactive monitoring allows administrators to quickly identify and respond to anomalies, such as repeated failed bind attempts or unauthorized modifications.

Implementing multi-factor authentication (MFA) for directory access, particularly for administrative accounts, is a highly recommended security control. By requiring a second form of verification, such as a hardware token, biometric factor, or mobile authenticator, MFA significantly reduces the risk of compromise even if LDAP credentials are leaked or stolen. While not all LDAP clients support native MFA, it is common to integrate LDAP with identity providers or VPN systems that enforce MFA at the point of user login.

Maintaining an up-to-date and hardened LDAP server is another critical best practice. Administrators should regularly apply security patches and updates provided by the LDAP server vendor to address known vulnerabilities and strengthen the server's defense against emerging threats. In addition, unnecessary services and modules should be disabled to reduce the attack surface. Default configurations, which may include insecure settings such as overly permissive ACLs or weak encryption ciphers, should be reviewed and adjusted according to the organization's security policies and best practices.

Secure configuration also extends to schema management. Unauthorized schema changes, such as the introduction of new object classes or attributes, can create security risks or inconsistencies in the directory structure. Schema modifications should be carefully controlled and reviewed by experienced administrators, and changes should be documented and version-controlled to maintain transparency and consistency across environments.

Another important consideration is securing replication traffic in LDAP environments that use multi-master or master-slave replication. Replication links should always be encrypted using SSL/TLS to prevent interception of sensitive data as it is synchronized between servers. Authentication between replication partners should be performed using strong service accounts with unique credentials, and replication traffic should be restricted to dedicated network segments whenever possible.

Segregation of LDAP servers into distinct tiers or roles can further enhance security. For example, external-facing LDAP servers used by web applications or public services should be separated from internal administrative servers that manage critical identity data. This separation limits the exposure of sensitive directory infrastructure to external threats and allows for more targeted security controls, such as firewalls, intrusion prevention systems, and network access control policies, to be applied to each tier.

Regular backup and disaster recovery procedures must also be part of an LDAP security strategy. Backups of the directory data, including configuration files and schema definitions, should be created frequently and stored securely, with encryption applied both at rest and in transit. Backup integrity should be tested regularly to ensure that data can be successfully restored in the event of hardware failure, corruption, or a ransomware attack.

Finally, user education and security awareness play a role in maintaining LDAP security. Users should be trained on password hygiene, social engineering risks, and how to recognize suspicious activity. Administrators and directory operators should receive specialized training on LDAP security principles, secure coding practices for LDAP-integrated applications, and incident response procedures specific to directory-related threats.

By adhering to LDAP security best practices, organizations can significantly reduce their exposure to cyberattacks and ensure the resilience and trustworthiness of their directory services. A secure LDAP environment underpins the broader identity and access management framework, enabling safe and reliable authentication and authorization processes across the enterprise. Strong encryption, strict access controls, continuous monitoring, and a proactive security culture form the foundation of protecting LDAP and the critical data it manages.

LDAP over SSL/TLS

LDAP over SSL/TLS is one of the most important security mechanisms used to protect directory services from unauthorized access and data interception. LDAP, by default, transmits all data, including usernames, passwords, and other sensitive information, in plain text over the network. This presents a significant security risk, especially in environments where data may traverse untrusted networks. By encapsulating LDAP traffic within a secure transport layer using SSL (Secure Sockets Layer) or its successor TLS (Transport Layer Security), organizations can ensure that directory communications are encrypted, preserving confidentiality and integrity while preventing eavesdropping and man-in-the-middle attacks.

The use of SSL/TLS with LDAP is typically implemented in two main ways: LDAP over SSL (LDAPS) and LDAP StartTLS. Both methods achieve the goal of encrypting LDAP communications, but they differ in how and when encryption is initiated during the session.

LDAP over SSL, commonly referred to as LDAPS, operates on TCP port 636 and establishes an encrypted session immediately upon connection. In this model, the client initiates a secure connection to the LDAP server before any LDAP protocol messages are exchanged. The entire session, from start to finish, is encrypted using SSL/TLS. This approach is straightforward and mirrors how HTTPS works for securing web traffic. LDAPS has been widely adopted in legacy environments and remains a standard option for securing LDAP traffic in many production systems. However, it is important to note that LDAPS requires a dedicated port separate from the default LDAP port 389, and server administrators must ensure that SSL/TLS certificates are properly installed and configured on the LDAP server to enable LDAPS functionality.

StartTLS, on the other hand, begins with an unencrypted connection over the standard LDAP port 389. After establishing the initial connection, the client sends an extended StartTLS request to the server, instructing it to upgrade the session to a secure SSL/TLS channel. If both the client and server support StartTLS and the handshake is successful, all subsequent LDAP operations are encrypted. The advantage of StartTLS is that it allows for both secure and non-secure traffic over the same port, offering greater flexibility for environments where legacy systems might still require non-encrypted LDAP access. StartTLS is also aligned with modern best practices recommended by standards bodies and is preferred in environments that require compatibility with multiple directory clients and servers.

Regardless of whether LDAPS or StartTLS is used, both methods rely on SSL/TLS certificates to establish trust between clients and servers. The LDAP server must present a valid digital certificate, typically signed by a trusted certificate authority (CA), during the SSL/TLS handshake. Clients verify the server's certificate to ensure that they are connecting to a legitimate and trusted directory service. Self-signed certificates may be used in closed environments or for testing purposes, but production systems should always use certificates issued by a recognized CA to avoid trust issues and potential vulnerabilities.

Proper certificate management is essential for maintaining secure LDAP connections. Certificates should be carefully monitored for expiration, and renewal processes should be automated or scheduled to prevent service interruptions. LDAP clients must also maintain an updated list of trusted root certificates to verify server certificates accurately. Certificate revocation mechanisms, such as Certificate Revocation Lists (CRLs) or Online Certificate Status Protocol (OCSP) responders, should be leveraged to ensure that revoked certificates are not accepted during the handshake process.

Another important consideration when implementing LDAP over SSL/TLS is the selection of secure cipher suites and protocol versions. Older versions of SSL, such as SSLv2 and SSLv3, are considered obsolete and vulnerable to multiple attack vectors, including the POODLE attack. Similarly, early versions of TLS, such as TLS 1.0 and TLS 1.1, have known weaknesses and should be disabled on both clients and servers. The industry standard is to use TLS 1.2 or TLS 1.3, which provide stronger encryption algorithms and improved handshake efficiency. Administrators should review their LDAP server configurations to enforce the use of strong cipher suites and the latest secure TLS protocols, reducing the risk of cryptographic vulnerabilities.

In addition to encrypting the LDAP traffic itself, SSL/TLS also protects sensitive operations such as user authentication. When LDAP is used to authenticate users in applications, VPNs, or other services, the bind operation typically involves transmitting user passwords. Without encryption, these passwords could be captured by an attacker monitoring network traffic. LDAP over SSL/TLS mitigates this risk by ensuring that credentials are securely transmitted, preserving the confidentiality of user passwords and other sensitive data during authentication processes.

LDAP replication traffic, which synchronizes directory data between master and replica servers, should also be secured using SSL/TLS. Replication processes involve transmitting full directory entries, including sensitive user information and sometimes even hashed passwords. By encrypting replication traffic, organizations can prevent unauthorized access to directory data as it moves between servers. In environments that implement multi-master replication or cross-site replication between geographically separated data centers, encrypting this traffic is even more critical to prevent interception over wide area networks or untrusted links.

Performance considerations must also be taken into account when enabling SSL/TLS on LDAP servers. While encryption introduces additional processing overhead due to the cryptographic operations involved in securing traffic, modern hardware and optimized cryptographic libraries reduce this impact significantly. However, administrators should monitor server load and performance metrics to ensure that the addition of SSL/TLS encryption does not adversely affect directory response times or availability, particularly under high query volumes.

In some cases, organizations deploy hardware security modules (HSMs) to offload cryptographic operations from LDAP servers, providing hardware-accelerated SSL/TLS encryption and stronger protection for private keys. HSMs are commonly used in environments with stringent security requirements, such as financial institutions or government agencies, where regulatory standards mandate the use of dedicated cryptographic hardware for securing critical infrastructure.

Securing LDAP traffic with SSL/TLS also helps meet regulatory and compliance requirements. Frameworks such as GDPR, HIPAA, and PCI DSS mandate the protection of sensitive data in transit, and using LDAP over SSL/TLS is a clear step toward meeting these obligations. Failure to implement proper encryption could expose organizations to data breaches and compliance violations, leading to financial penalties and reputational damage.

Finally, LDAP over SSL/TLS should be regularly tested and audited to ensure that security configurations remain effective over time. Regular vulnerability assessments and penetration tests should include LDAP services as part of their scope, verifying that encryption is enforced, certificates are valid and strong ciphers are used. Any misconfigurations, such as fallback to unencrypted connections or acceptance of weak protocol versions, should be remediated promptly to maintain a robust security posture.

LDAP over SSL/TLS is not simply an optional enhancement but a fundamental requirement for securing directory services in modern IT environments. By enforcing encryption for all LDAP communications, organizations can protect the sensitive identity and access data that flows through their infrastructure, safeguarding against threats while enabling trusted and secure identity management operations across the enterprise.

Using SASL with LDAP

Using SASL with LDAP adds a flexible and secure authentication layer to directory services, extending beyond the capabilities of basic simple bind operations. SASL, which stands for Simple Authentication and

Security Layer, is a framework that allows LDAP clients and servers to negotiate various authentication mechanisms and security layers dynamically. This abstraction provides LDAP implementations with the ability to support a wide variety of authentication protocols without being tied to a single method. The result is a more adaptable and extensible directory service capable of meeting diverse authentication and security requirements.

The SASL framework separates the authentication mechanism from the LDAP protocol itself, meaning that the LDAP server does not need to know the specifics of each mechanism ahead of time. Instead, SASL mechanisms are negotiated during the bind process. Clients and servers use SASL to establish the method for authenticating a session and optionally negotiate security layers that add encryption or integrity protection to LDAP traffic. By supporting SASL, an LDAP server can offer multiple authentication options simultaneously, such as Kerberos, DIGEST-MD5, EXTERNAL certificate-based authentication, or PLAIN with TLS protection.

One of the most common SASL mechanisms used with LDAP is GSSAPI, which is typically associated with Kerberos authentication. In environments where Kerberos infrastructure is in place, GSSAPI allows LDAP clients to authenticate using Kerberos tickets, providing single sign-on capabilities across systems and services. A client authenticates to the Kerberos Key Distribution Center (KDC) to obtain a ticket-granting ticket (TGT) and then uses it to request a service ticket for the LDAP server. This service ticket is presented to the LDAP server via the SASL GSSAPI mechanism during the bind operation. The LDAP server validates the ticket with the KDC, and upon successful verification, the user is authenticated without sending a password over the network. This integration strengthens security by eliminating password transmission and supports mutual authentication, ensuring that both the client and server verify each other's identities.

Another widely used SASL mechanism is DIGEST-MD5. This challenge-response authentication protocol improves upon simple bind authentication by preventing the transmission of passwords in clear text. During a DIGEST-MD5 exchange, the LDAP server sends a nonce to the client, and the client responds by hashing its credentials along with the nonce and other session parameters. This hash is then sent to the server for verification. DIGEST-MD5 provides basic protection against replay and eavesdropping attacks, although it has largely been superseded by stronger mechanisms such as SCRAM (Salted Challenge Response Authentication Mechanism) and GSSAPI in modern deployments.

The EXTERNAL mechanism is another important SASL method used in conjunction with LDAP. EXTERNAL leverages credentials provided by an external source, typically a TLS client certificate, to authenticate the user. When a client connects to the LDAP server over a TLS-secured session and presents a valid client certificate, the server uses the EXTERNAL SASL mechanism to map the certificate to a user identity in the directory. This form of authentication is particularly useful for automated systems, service accounts, or environments that require certificate-based trust without relying on passwords or tickets. It is also common in scenarios where organizations enforce PKI-based security policies.

The PLAIN SASL mechanism transmits the user's credentials in clear text as part of the authentication exchange. While this may seem insecure, it is often used in environments where LDAP communications are already encrypted using SSL/TLS, which protects the credentials during transmission. PLAIN is valued for its simplicity and ease of implementation but should never be used without SSL/TLS to ensure credentials are not exposed to network attackers.

When configuring SASL for LDAP, both the server and client must support the same mechanisms. The list of available SASL mechanisms is typically defined by the SASL implementation installed on the LDAP server. For example, OpenLDAP integrates with Cyrus SASL, a popular SASL library that supports numerous mechanisms, including GSSAPI, DIGEST-MD5, PLAIN, SCRAM, and EXTERNAL. Administrators can configure which mechanisms to enable or disable based on the organization's security requirements and infrastructure.

SASL mechanisms can also include negotiated security layers that go beyond authentication. Once a SASL bind is successful, some mechanisms allow the client and server to agree on additional protections, such as integrity checks (data signing) or encryption (data privacy). This adds an extra security layer on top of the authentication, ensuring that LDAP traffic is protected against tampering or interception, even if SSL/TLS is not used. However, in modern deployments, SSL/TLS is still commonly employed alongside SASL to secure LDAP sessions.

The integration of SASL with LDAP also enables proxy authorization, where one user or service acts on behalf of another identity. The proxy authorization control is used alongside SASL mechanisms to allow an authenticated client to specify an alternate authorization identity. For example, an application could authenticate using a service account and then perform LDAP operations on behalf of an end user by specifying the user's DN in the proxy authorization control. This capability is useful in application servers, middleware platforms, or identity management systems where centralized services need to act on behalf of multiple users without managing separate credentials for each user session.

SASL also provides interoperability benefits, as it enables LDAP servers to participate in broader authentication ecosystems. For instance, organizations that use Kerberos for centralized authentication can integrate LDAP seamlessly using GSSAPI, aligning directory services with existing identity infrastructures. Similarly, environments that employ TLS mutual authentication can leverage EXTERNAL to authenticate LDAP clients based on certificates issued by a corporate certificate authority.

When deploying SASL with LDAP, security best practices must be followed to ensure robust protection. Administrators should disable weaker or outdated mechanisms, such as ANONYMOUS or deprecated challenge-response protocols, unless explicitly required for legacy compatibility. Configuration files for SASL libraries and LDAP servers should be reviewed to enforce the use of strong, modern authentication protocols and to restrict unauthorized clients from negotiating insecure mechanisms.

SASL authentication also impacts the way access control and permissions are enforced within the directory. Once an LDAP session is authenticated using a SASL mechanism, the bind DN or authorization identity established during the process is used to evaluate access control rules. For example, a user authenticated via

GSSAPI will be mapped to a specific DN in the directory, and their permissions will be evaluated against Access Control Lists (ACLs) based on that DN. This ensures consistent enforcement of security policies regardless of the authentication method used.

SASL integration with LDAP is critical for organizations that require flexible, scalable, and secure authentication methods across heterogeneous environments. It empowers administrators to choose authentication mechanisms that best align with organizational policies, technical requirements, and regulatory obligations. By supporting mechanisms such as GSSAPI, EXTERNAL, and DIGEST-MD5, SASL strengthens LDAP's position as a versatile and secure component in enterprise identity and access management architectures. Whether deployed to enable single sign-on with Kerberos, certificate-based authentication, or simple password validation over secure channels, SASL provides the foundation for modernizing LDAP authentication processes while maintaining high levels of security and interoperability.

Troubleshooting LDAP Issues

Troubleshooting LDAP issues is an essential skill for administrators who manage directory services in any organization. LDAP is a critical component of many IT infrastructures, providing authentication, authorization, and directory services for a wide range of applications and systems. However, due to its complexity and the many dependencies involved in its operation, LDAP problems can arise at multiple layers, from client misconfigurations to network-related issues, schema errors, and access control misalignments. Resolving these problems requires a systematic approach that includes understanding the LDAP protocol, interpreting error messages, and using appropriate diagnostic tools to isolate and fix the root causes.

The first step in troubleshooting LDAP is to clearly define the nature of the issue. LDAP-related problems may manifest as authentication failures, inability to query or modify directory data, slow response times, or replication inconsistencies. Pinpointing the exact symptoms helps narrow down potential causes. For example, if users report failed logins, the issue could be related to bind failures, expired passwords, or incorrect credentials. If an application cannot retrieve user data, the root cause might lie in search filter misconfigurations, permission issues, or schema constraints. Gathering error messages from logs, user reports, or application output provides essential clues to guide further investigation.

Authentication failures are among the most common LDAP issues and often relate to bind operations. When troubleshooting failed binds, administrators should first verify the credentials being used, ensuring that the username is formatted correctly, typically as a fully qualified distinguished name. A common mistake is to supply a short username, such as jdoe, instead of the full DN, such as uid=jdoe,ou=users,dc=example,dc=com. If the credentials are correct, the next step is to examine access control lists to ensure that the account has sufficient permissions to bind to the server. Additionally, bind failures may result from locked accounts, expired passwords, or incorrect LDAP service account configurations in applications.

Network-related problems are another frequent source of LDAP issues. Since LDAP operates over TCP/IP, troubleshooting should always include checking basic network connectivity between the client and the LDAP server. Tools such as ping and traceroute can be used to verify that the client can reach the server's IP address, while telnet or nc (netcat) can test whether the appropriate LDAP port, such as 389 for standard LDAP or 636 for LDAPS, is accessible. Firewalls, load balancers, or network access control lists may block traffic to or from the LDAP server, preventing clients from establishing sessions. Network issues can also include DNS misconfigurations, where clients fail to resolve the server's hostname correctly, leading to failed connections.

LDAP encryption-related issues can occur when using LDAPS or StartTLS. These problems often result from certificate errors, such as expired server certificates, mismatched hostnames, or untrusted certificate authorities. Clients may reject the server's certificate if the certificate does not match the hostname being used in the connection or if the client's trust store lacks the necessary CA certificate. Diagnosing these issues involves reviewing SSL/TLS handshake logs, which can be enabled with verbose logging options in most LDAP clients. Running openssl s_client -connect ldap.example.com:636 is a common technique to test SSL/TLS connectivity and validate that the certificate chain is correct and trusted.

Search and query failures are another area where LDAP issues frequently arise. LDAP search operations require a valid base DN, scope, and filter. If an application or script specifies an incorrect base DN, the LDAP server may return no results or an error indicating that the search base could not be found. Similarly, an overly broad or malformed search filter can result in performance issues or unexpected results. For example, using (objectClass=*) on a large subtree can cause timeouts or excessive server load. Troubleshooting these problems involves validating the search parameters and testing them using command-line tools like ldapsearch, which allows administrators to replicate the query outside of the application and adjust the filter syntax or scope as needed.

Access control issues, governed by LDAP's ACLs, can prevent users or applications from performing certain operations, such as reading, writing, or modifying directory entries. If a user cannot access a specific attribute or entry, administrators should review the directory's ACL configuration to determine whether the bind identity has the necessary permissions. It is common for ACLs to restrict sensitive attributes like userPassword, telephone numbers, or group memberships to prevent unauthorized access. Reviewing server logs will often reveal denied operations, with details about the DN used, the attempted operation, and the specific ACL rule that blocked the request.

Replication problems can also disrupt LDAP services, particularly in environments that rely on multi-master or master-slave replication. Symptoms of replication issues include data inconsistencies between servers, missing entries, or replication delays. Administrators should first check replication logs for errors related to synchronization, schema mismatches, or authentication failures between replication partners. Common replication issues involve improper replication filters, incompatible schema configurations, or conflicts arising from concurrent updates on different servers. Tools like slapcat and slaptest in OpenLDAP environments can be used to validate the integrity of directory data and configurations, while replication status commands provide real-time information about the state of replication agreements.

Performance degradation is another area that requires troubleshooting, especially in directories that handle a high volume of queries. Slow responses may stem from insufficient indexing of frequently queried attributes, such as uid, mail, or cn. Without appropriate indexes, the LDAP server may perform full table scans on large datasets, leading to delays. Administrators should review the server's indexing configuration and monitor query patterns to identify which attributes are most frequently used in search filters. Adjusting indexes and optimizing queries can significantly improve performance.

Schema violations can cause LDAP operations to fail, particularly when adding or modifying entries. If an attribute is missing or if a value does not conform to the attribute's defined syntax, the server will reject the operation with a schema violation error. Troubleshooting schema issues involves comparing the object classes and attributes of the problematic entry against the directory schema. Schema extension errors may occur when new custom attributes or object classes are introduced but not consistently applied across all servers, especially in replicated environments.

Finally, enabling verbose logging and diagnostic modes is crucial during the troubleshooting process. Most LDAP servers, including OpenLDAP, support multiple log levels that can be adjusted to capture detailed information about client connections, operations, and internal processing. Logs should be examined systematically to identify patterns, such as recurring error codes or failed operations linked to specific clients or accounts. Common LDAP error codes, such as invalidCredentials (code 49), insufficientAccessRights (code 50), or noSuchObject (code 32), provide valuable insights into the nature of the problem and should be cross-referenced with official LDAP documentation for further context.

Troubleshooting LDAP issues requires a structured, methodical approach that addresses the full stack of potential problems, from client-side misconfigurations to network constraints and server-side limitations. Mastery of diagnostic tools like ldapsearch, ldapmodify, and openssl, combined with careful log analysis and a solid understanding of LDAP operations, empowers administrators to resolve problems efficiently and ensure the stability and reliability of directory services across their environments.

LDAP Performance Tuning

LDAP performance tuning is a critical aspect of maintaining a responsive and reliable directory service, particularly in large-scale environments where thousands or even millions of directory queries and operations may occur each day. An efficiently tuned LDAP server ensures that authentication, search, and modification requests are processed quickly, reducing application latency and improving the user experience across dependent systems. Directory performance can be influenced by several factors, including hardware resources, server configuration, indexing strategies, access control design, and network conditions. Successful performance tuning requires a holistic approach that balances these variables to achieve optimal throughput and minimal response times.

One of the foundational elements of LDAP performance tuning is the appropriate use of indexing. LDAP servers maintain indexes on directory attributes to speed up search operations. Without indexes, the server would need to perform a full directory scan to process search filters, leading to unacceptable delays, especially in directories with large datasets. Administrators must analyze the most frequently used search filters in their environment and ensure that attributes such as uid, cn, mail, objectClass, and member are properly indexed. The selection of indexes should reflect the search patterns of both end users and applications. For instance, if a web portal commonly queries the directory for users by their email address, indexing the mail attribute is essential for efficient lookups.

Beyond selecting which attributes to index, administrators must also configure the appropriate index types. Common index types include equality indexes, which optimize searches for exact matches, and presence indexes, which improve searches checking for the existence of an attribute. Substring indexes support wildcard searches but can significantly increase the size and complexity of index files, so they should be used selectively. Balancing index coverage with storage and memory considerations is key, as over-indexing may result in excessive disk I/O and higher memory consumption during index maintenance.

Memory allocation is another core component of LDAP performance tuning. LDAP servers rely heavily on available RAM to cache directory data and indexes, reducing the need for disk access and accelerating query responses. Administrators should allocate sufficient memory to the LDAP process and its caching mechanisms, such as the entry cache and database cache. For example, in OpenLDAP, the olcDbCacheSize parameter controls the number of directory entries that can be held in memory, while olcDbIDLcacheSize determines the number of index ID lists cached. The goal is to size these caches to fit the working set of directory data into memory, minimizing the performance penalty of disk reads.

Tuning the LDAP server's threading model can further enhance performance, especially in environments with high concurrent traffic. LDAP servers handle multiple client connections simultaneously using a pool of worker threads. Configuring the number of threads appropriately helps prevent bottlenecks under heavy loads. Too few threads may cause requests to queue, increasing latency, while too many threads can overwhelm the server's CPU and memory. Administrators should monitor metrics such as CPU utilization, thread wait times, and connection queues to determine the optimal thread pool size for their specific workload.

Network latency and bandwidth are also important considerations in LDAP performance tuning. Directory services that span multiple geographic regions or operate over wide area networks (WANs) may experience delays due to network round-trip times. To mitigate these effects, organizations can deploy LDAP replicas closer to end users, reducing the distance queries must travel. Load balancers and Global Server Load Balancing (GSLB) solutions can help direct client requests to the nearest LDAP server, improving response times and distributing traffic evenly across available nodes.

Replication performance can also impact the overall efficiency of LDAP environments. In multi-master or master-slave replication setups, ensuring timely synchronization of directory changes is crucial to maintaining data consistency across servers. Administrators should configure replication intervals and filters to match business requirements. For example, real-time or continuous replication may be necessary for mission-critical services, while less frequent synchronization might suffice for read-only replicas in remote offices. Additionally, replication traffic should be secured and optimized, using compression if available, to reduce the impact on network performance.

Access Control Lists, while critical for securing directory data, can also affect performance if not carefully designed. Complex ACLs with multiple rules and conditions may increase the processing overhead for each LDAP operation, particularly for search requests that involve large result sets. Simplifying ACL structures, minimizing the number of conditional checks, and applying rules at higher directory tree levels can reduce the time required for access control evaluation. Administrators should periodically review and streamline ACL configurations, ensuring that they provide necessary security without unnecessarily degrading performance.

Another performance consideration is connection management. Some applications and services may open and close LDAP connections frequently, causing additional overhead for session setup and teardown. Implementing connection pooling, where clients reuse established LDAP connections instead of creating new ones for each operation, can significantly improve performance by reducing connection churn. Most LDAP client libraries and middleware platforms support connection pooling features that can be tuned based on expected load and application behavior.

Periodic database maintenance is also a best practice for sustained LDAP performance. Over time, directory databases can become fragmented or accumulate stale entries, leading to inefficiencies. Scheduled database compaction, reindexing, and cleanup tasks help maintain optimal data structures and reduce the likelihood of performance degradation. In OpenLDAP environments, tools like slapindex and slapcat can be used to regenerate indexes and export directory data, while database tuning parameters in the underlying storage backend, such as Berkeley DB or LMDB, should be adjusted to optimize I/O patterns.

Monitoring and benchmarking are critical components of any performance tuning initiative. Administrators should implement continuous monitoring to track key performance indicators such as query response times, CPU and memory utilization, connection counts, replication latency, and disk I/O. Tools like ldapsearch, custom scripts, and dedicated monitoring platforms can provide valuable insights into how the LDAP server is performing under various conditions. Benchmarking tools, such as SLAMD or custom load-testing scripts, allow administrators to simulate production-like workloads and evaluate the effects of configuration changes before deploying them to live environments.

Finally, hardware and virtualization considerations play a role in LDAP performance. LDAP servers benefit from fast disks, such as SSDs, to reduce storage latency for database files and transaction logs. In virtualized environments, LDAP servers should be provisioned with dedicated CPU and memory resources to avoid contention with other virtual machines. Ensuring that LDAP servers operate on stable, low-latency networks and have access to high-performance storage infrastructure supports the overall goal of providing rapid, reliable directory services to users and applications.

LDAP performance tuning is a continuous process that requires a deep understanding of the directory workload, user behavior, and system architecture. By combining thoughtful configuration of indexing, caching, threading, replication, access control, and hardware optimization, administrators can deliver a directory service that scales with organizational growth, maintains high availability, and responds quickly to the authentication and data retrieval needs of modern applications.

LDAP Backup and Recovery

LDAP backup and recovery are fundamental components of directory service administration, ensuring business continuity and safeguarding critical identity and access data against corruption, accidental deletion, or catastrophic failures. The LDAP directory often contains sensitive and essential information such as user accounts, passwords, access control policies, group memberships, and organizational hierarchies. This data supports the authentication and authorization processes for a wide range of applications and systems. Therefore, implementing a reliable backup and recovery strategy is essential for any organization that relies on LDAP services for daily operations.

The first aspect of LDAP backup involves determining what needs to be backed up. LDAP directories consist of two primary elements: the directory data and the server configuration. Directory data includes all the entries stored within the Directory Information Tree, such as user objects, groups, and other resources. The server configuration encompasses schema definitions, access control lists, logging settings, and other operational parameters that define how the directory server functions. A comprehensive backup strategy should include both elements to ensure that the entire LDAP environment can be fully restored in case of a disaster.

One of the most common methods for backing up LDAP data is through the use of LDIF, the LDAP Data Interchange Format. LDIF is a plain-text format that represents directory entries in a standardized, portable way. Tools like slapcat in OpenLDAP environments allow administrators to export the entire directory or specific subtrees into an LDIF file. The slapcat utility reads the backend database directly, bypassing the LDAP protocol, and creates a point-in-time snapshot of the directory content. This approach is efficient and widely used because it does not require the LDAP server to be stopped, allowing administrators to perform backups during normal operation.

In addition to slapcat, the ldapsearch command can be used to generate LDIF backups, especially when administrators need to export specific branches of the directory. While ldapsearch performs the export through the LDAP protocol itself, which can be slower than direct backend access, it provides more granular control over search filters and scopes. For instance, ldapsearch can be used to export only user entries within a particular organizational unit or to exclude certain attributes from the backup file.

Backing up the directory data alone is not sufficient. LDAP server configurations and schema files must also be backed up to ensure a full recovery. In OpenLDAP, configuration data is often stored in the cn=config directory, which itself is represented as an LDAP directory tree. This configuration database can be exported to LDIF using the slapcat utility with a target base DN of cn=config. The resulting LDIF file captures the entire server configuration, including database settings, ACLs, module load instructions, and schema extensions. Maintaining backups of this configuration directory allows administrators to restore the exact server settings in the event of a failure or to replicate configurations across multiple LDAP servers.

Once the backup files are generated, they should be stored securely and replicated to multiple locations, such as off-site storage or cloud backup systems. Backup files may contain sensitive information, including user credentials and internal organizational structures, so encryption of the backups at rest and during transit is strongly recommended. Administrators should use tools that support encrypted storage or apply encryption mechanisms such as GPG or native filesystem encryption to protect the backup files from unauthorized access.

Recovery procedures begin with assessing the scope of the failure. If only individual entries or subtrees are lost or corrupted, administrators may opt to perform a targeted recovery by re-importing specific entries from an LDIF backup. Using the ldapadd or ldapmodify tools, administrators can selectively restore affected portions of the directory without disrupting the entire environment. This approach is commonly used in scenarios where an administrator accidentally deletes a user or group or when a configuration change inadvertently removes access to certain directory entries.

For full directory recovery, the server's backend database may need to be recreated. In OpenLDAP, this involves stopping the LDAP service, clearing the backend database files, and using the slapadd utility to load the backup LDIF file into the backend. The slapadd command directly inserts directory entries into the database, bypassing normal LDAP processing, and is typically faster than using ldapadd for bulk imports. After the data is restored, administrators should regenerate indexes using slapindex to ensure optimal search performance. Once the database is fully rebuilt and indexed, the LDAP service can be restarted, and functionality validated.

Recovery of server configurations follows a similar process. The cn=config directory can be restored from its backup LDIF file using slapadd with the -no option, which targets the configuration database. Care must be taken when restoring configurations, as incorrect or incomplete configuration files can prevent the LDAP server from starting properly. Administrators should carefully review the configuration LDIF and apply necessary adjustments to reflect the current environment, such as server hostnames, TLS certificates, or database paths, before initiating the restore.

In replicated LDAP environments, such as multi-master or master-slave setups, recovery procedures must also address replication consistency. After restoring a replica server from backup, it is crucial to verify that the server can successfully rejoin the replication topology and synchronize with its peers. In cases where the restored replica contains outdated data, administrators may need to reinitialize replication by performing a full resync from a trusted master server.

Testing and documentation are essential elements of a successful LDAP backup and recovery strategy. Regularly scheduled recovery drills ensure that backup files are valid and that administrators are familiar with recovery procedures. These drills should simulate realistic scenarios, such as restoring after hardware failures, database corruption, or ransomware attacks. Documenting each step of the backup and recovery process helps ensure consistency, reduces errors during emergency situations, and provides a valuable reference for new team members or external auditors.

Automation can further enhance LDAP backup and recovery workflows. Administrators can schedule periodic exports using cron jobs or similar task schedulers, ensuring that backups are performed regularly without manual intervention. Automated scripts can include pre- and post-backup validation checks, such as verifying the integrity of the backup file, encrypting the output, and rotating older backups according to the organization's retention policy.

A robust LDAP backup and recovery strategy not only protects directory data but also supports compliance with regulatory frameworks and industry standards. Regulations such as GDPR, HIPAA, and ISO 27001 emphasize the importance of protecting personal data and maintaining service availability, making reliable backups a key element of an organization's overall security and disaster recovery posture. By implementing comprehensive backup and recovery practices, organizations can safeguard the continuity of their identity and access management systems, minimize downtime, and ensure that directory services remain available and secure under any circumstances.

High Availability for LDAP

High availability for LDAP is essential to ensure continuous and uninterrupted access to directory services, which are critical to supporting authentication, authorization, and user directory lookups across enterprise applications and infrastructure. LDAP directories often serve as the backbone of identity management, enabling login processes, access controls, and user provisioning for a variety of dependent services. Any outage or degradation of the directory service can result in widespread disruptions, leaving users unable to log in to applications, access network resources, or perform essential tasks. To mitigate these risks, organizations implement high availability (HA) strategies that minimize downtime and increase resilience against hardware failures, network outages, or software crashes.

The foundation of LDAP high availability is redundancy. Deploying multiple LDAP servers within the infrastructure ensures that if one server fails, others can continue to handle client requests. Redundant LDAP servers can be configured in several ways, depending on the organization's requirements and the complexity of its environment. A common approach is to implement a master-slave replication model, where a single master LDAP server handles all write operations, while one or more read-only replicas or consumers serve read requests. If the master becomes unavailable, the replicas can continue to process read requests, maintaining partial service availability until the master is restored.

Another popular high availability model is multi-master replication, where two or more LDAP servers function as peers, each capable of handling both read and write operations. Multi-master replication increases fault tolerance by allowing clients to direct writes to any available server, ensuring that directory updates can continue even if one of the servers fails. Changes made to any of the servers are synchronized with the others, typically using real-time or near-real-time replication. While this model provides higher availability, it also introduces complexity, as administrators must manage conflict resolution and ensure consistency across the replicated servers.

Load balancing is a critical component of high availability for LDAP, enabling client connections to be distributed across multiple servers. Load balancers can be implemented using hardware appliances, virtualized load balancers, or software-based solutions like HAProxy or NGINX. A load balancer acts as a single access point for LDAP clients, directing queries to available backend servers based on configured algorithms such as round-robin, least connections, or geographic proximity. Load balancers can also perform health checks to ensure that client traffic is only routed to servers that are operational and responsive. If a server fails a health check, the load balancer automatically removes it from the pool until it is restored.

DNS-based strategies can complement load balancing to enhance LDAP availability. By configuring DNS round-robin entries for LDAP servers, clients can be directed to different servers based on DNS responses. This approach provides a basic level of distribution, although it lacks the health checking and failover capabilities of dedicated load balancers. Alternatively, some organizations use Global Server Load Balancing (GSLB) to direct clients to the nearest LDAP server based on geographic location or latency, improving both availability and performance for users in different regions.

Replication design is a key factor in achieving LDAP high availability. Administrators must carefully plan the replication topology, ensuring that data is synchronized efficiently between servers while minimizing the risk of conflicts or replication bottlenecks. In multi-master environments, proper conflict resolution mechanisms must be in place, often relying on timestamp-based logic where the most recent change takes precedence. For large-scale deployments, administrators may create replication hubs that aggregate updates from multiple servers before distributing them to other replicas, reducing the load on individual nodes.

To further enhance LDAP availability, some organizations implement failover clustering, where LDAP servers are deployed as part of a high-availability cluster. In a failover cluster, a secondary server is configured to automatically take over the role of a failed primary server, ensuring that directory services remain available with minimal disruption. Clustering solutions typically include shared storage and heartbeat mechanisms to detect server failures and trigger automatic failover processes. While clustering increases resilience, it may require specialized hardware, software, and careful configuration to avoid split-brain scenarios, where two servers simultaneously attempt to assume the primary role.

Disaster recovery planning is also a fundamental aspect of LDAP high availability. In addition to local redundancy, organizations should maintain geographically distributed LDAP servers to protect against site-wide failures, such as natural disasters, power outages, or network disruptions affecting a specific data center. By replicating directory data to remote sites and configuring DNS or load balancer failover mechanisms, organizations can maintain directory services even in the event of a complete site failure. Regularly testing disaster recovery procedures ensures that the failover process works as intended and that recovery times meet the organization's business continuity objectives.

High availability for LDAP also requires attention to data consistency and integrity. Replication alone does not guarantee that all servers will have identical data at all times, particularly in environments with high write volumes or frequent schema updates. Administrators should monitor replication status closely, review logs for replication errors, and implement automated alerts to detect synchronization delays or failures. Performing periodic consistency checks between replicas helps identify discrepancies and enables corrective actions, such as re-synchronizing servers or performing manual reconciliations.

Security is another key consideration in high availability designs. All replication and client-server communications should be secured using SSL/TLS to protect data in transit. Load balancers should be configured to pass client certificates when using TLS client authentication or SASL EXTERNAL mechanisms. Additionally, LDAP servers should enforce strict access controls to limit administrative operations to authorized personnel, reducing the risk of accidental or malicious actions that could impact availability.

Monitoring and alerting tools play a critical role in maintaining high availability for LDAP. Administrators should implement monitoring solutions that track key metrics such as server uptime, query response times, replication latency, and system resource utilization. Tools like Prometheus, Nagios, or Zabbix can provide real-time insights and generate alerts when performance thresholds are breached or when service outages occur. Coupled with centralized logging and analysis platforms, monitoring enables proactive identification of potential issues before they escalate into outages.

Capacity planning is another essential component of LDAP high availability. As organizations grow, LDAP query volumes and write operations may increase, placing additional strain on directory servers. Administrators should forecast growth trends and scale the LDAP infrastructure accordingly, adding additional servers or upgrading hardware resources to accommodate increased demand. Proactive capacity management reduces the risk of performance degradation or service interruptions caused by resource exhaustion.

High availability for LDAP is not achieved solely through technology; it also relies on operational readiness and procedural discipline. Administrators should document high availability designs, replication topologies, and failover procedures, ensuring that all team members understand how to maintain and troubleshoot the infrastructure. Regular training, simulation exercises, and post-incident reviews help strengthen the organization's ability to respond effectively to LDAP service disruptions.

By implementing high availability strategies that combine redundancy, replication, load balancing, disaster recovery, and monitoring, organizations can ensure that their LDAP directories remain available and resilient. This supports the continuous operation of critical business functions, protects against data loss, and provides a stable foundation for identity and access management across enterprise environments.

LDAP Logging and Monitoring

LDAP logging and monitoring are essential practices for maintaining the health, security, and performance of directory services. An LDAP directory acts as the central repository for authentication, authorization, and identity data in many organizations. Therefore, understanding how the service behaves, how it is accessed, and how it performs under load is crucial for ensuring its availability and reliability. Logging provides a detailed record of the directory server's operations, while monitoring offers real-time visibility into system metrics, resource usage, and potential anomalies. Together, these practices help administrators troubleshoot issues, detect security incidents, and optimize LDAP server performance.

LDAP logging captures information about client connections, bind attempts, search queries, modify operations, replication events, and internal server processes. Most LDAP servers, including OpenLDAP and Microsoft Active Directory, provide configurable logging facilities that allow administrators to define which events are recorded and at what level of detail. For example, OpenLDAP uses log levels that range from basic connection logs to verbose debugging output, such as logs that show each LDAP request, search filter, or access control decision. By adjusting the log level, administrators can balance the need for detailed information with the overhead and storage requirements associated with generating large log files.

One of the primary uses of LDAP logs is security auditing. Logs capture authentication events, such as successful and failed bind attempts, allowing administrators to detect brute-force attacks, unauthorized access attempts, or compromised accounts. Each bind operation recorded in the logs typically includes the DN used, the client IP address, a timestamp, and the result code. Monitoring these entries helps identify suspicious patterns, such as repeated failed logins from a single IP address or unexpected authentication attempts from foreign networks. LDAP logs also reveal who accessed specific directory objects and whether they performed read, write, or delete operations, which is vital for auditing sensitive changes and maintaining compliance with data protection regulations.

Monitoring LDAP server performance is equally important. Directory servers handle large volumes of queries and write operations, especially in enterprise environments with thousands of users and multiple integrated systems. Administrators must continuously monitor key performance indicators (KPIs) such as CPU and memory utilization, disk I/O, query response times, and connection counts to ensure that the directory service operates within acceptable thresholds. When performance metrics exceed defined baselines, such as high CPU spikes or increased query latency, administrators can proactively investigate the root cause and implement corrective actions before users are impacted.

LDAP monitoring also involves observing connection patterns and session lifecycles. Applications and clients that create excessive or short-lived connections may degrade server performance by consuming unnecessary resources. By monitoring connection rates and durations, administrators can detect inefficient client behaviors and recommend best practices such as connection pooling. Additionally, high numbers of concurrent connections may indicate a surge in legitimate user activity or, conversely, a potential denial-of-service attack against the directory.

Replication monitoring is critical in environments where LDAP servers synchronize data across multiple nodes. Monitoring replication status ensures that changes made on one server propagate to all replicas in a timely manner, preserving data consistency across the infrastructure. Administrators should track replication delays, conflict resolution events, and the status of replication agreements. In OpenLDAP, replication logs generated by syncrepl or delta-syncrepl processes provide insights into synchronization activity, including connection states between providers and consumers and details of data updates. Failure to detect replication issues early can lead to data divergence, resulting in inconsistent user accounts, broken access policies, or stale directory records.

Centralized log aggregation and analysis tools greatly enhance LDAP logging and monitoring capabilities. By forwarding LDAP logs to platforms such as the ELK Stack (Elasticsearch, Logstash, Kibana), Splunk, or Graylog, administrators can correlate directory events with logs from other systems, visualize trends, and build dashboards that provide a comprehensive view of LDAP service health and security. These platforms enable advanced queries, alerting mechanisms, and long-term log retention, supporting both operational troubleshooting and regulatory compliance reporting.

For security-conscious organizations, LDAP logs can be integrated with Security Information and Event Management (SIEM) systems. This integration allows for automated detection of suspicious patterns, such as unusual login hours, privilege escalation attempts, or unauthorized schema modifications. SIEM systems can trigger real-time alerts based on defined rules and workflows, enabling rapid incident response to mitigate potential security breaches.

Proper log management is essential to prevent logging from impacting LDAP server performance or overwhelming disk storage. Administrators should configure log rotation policies to archive or delete older log files periodically, using tools such as logrotate on Linux systems. Logs should be compressed to reduce storage consumption and encrypted if stored in locations where sensitive data must be protected. Retention policies should align with organizational policies and regulatory requirements, ensuring that logs are available for audit purposes for the required duration.

Proactive LDAP monitoring also involves tracking service uptime and availability. Tools such as Nagios, Zabbix, or Prometheus can be configured to monitor LDAP service ports, simulate authentication or search operations, and alert administrators in the event of service degradation or downtime. These tools can check for specific error codes returned by LDAP servers, such as referral errors, unavailable replicas, or resource exhaustion, allowing teams to address issues before they escalate into full outages.

In addition to monitoring system-level and application-level metrics, LDAP administrators should observe schema-related changes and administrative operations. Unauthorized modifications to schema files or changes to Access Control Lists can have wide-ranging effects on directory integrity and security. Regular audits of schema and configuration changes, combined with careful monitoring of administrative access, help maintain the stability and trustworthiness of the LDAP environment.

High-level monitoring also includes capacity planning. By analyzing trends in query volumes, connection counts, and resource usage over time, administrators can anticipate future growth and make informed decisions about scaling the LDAP infrastructure. This might involve adding additional replicas, upgrading server hardware, or optimizing server configurations to handle increasing demand without sacrificing performance or reliability.

LDAP logging and monitoring form the backbone of an effective directory service management strategy. They enable organizations to identify performance bottlenecks, detect and respond to security threats, ensure regulatory compliance, and deliver a high-quality user experience by maintaining a responsive and secure directory service. When combined with proper alerting, log management, and visualization tools, these practices empower administrators to manage LDAP environments proactively, reducing downtime and supporting business-critical identity and access management operations across diverse IT ecosystems.

LDAP in Cloud Environments

LDAP in cloud environments has become an increasingly common and essential component of modern IT infrastructure as organizations shift to hybrid and fully cloud-native models. While LDAP has traditionally been associated with on-premises directory services, its role is just as critical in the cloud, where identity and access management must extend across virtualized networks, applications, and services that are no longer confined to local data centers. In cloud environments, LDAP provides centralized user management, secure authentication, and support for a wide range of applications that depend on directory services for controlling access to resources.

One of the primary motivations for implementing LDAP in the cloud is the need to maintain a unified directory service that supports both cloud-based and on-premises applications. Many enterprises are adopting hybrid models, where some services remain in private data centers while others move to public cloud platforms such as Amazon Web Services, Microsoft Azure, or Google Cloud. In these environments, LDAP can act as a bridge, providing a common identity source that synchronizes user and group information across both domains. This allows users to authenticate with the same credentials regardless of whether they are accessing local applications or cloud-hosted services, reducing identity fragmentation and simplifying account management.

Cloud-hosted LDAP services are available through multiple vendors, offering managed directory platforms that reduce the operational burden of maintaining LDAP infrastructure. Services like AWS Directory Service for Microsoft Active Directory, Azure Active Directory Domain Services, and Google Cloud Directory Sync provide LDAP-compatible interfaces while abstracting much of the complexity of deployment, patching, scaling, and high availability. These managed solutions integrate directly with other cloud-native services, such as identity federation tools, access management platforms, and SaaS applications, enabling seamless identity integration across the enterprise.

For organizations that prefer to maintain greater control, self-hosting LDAP servers in cloud environments is also a viable option. Deploying OpenLDAP or other LDAP servers on virtual machines or containerized workloads allows administrators to customize configurations, apply custom schema extensions, and maintain full control over directory policies. These LDAP servers can be deployed in highly available architectures using cloud-native tools such as auto-scaling groups, load balancers, and multi-zone deployments to ensure resilience and scalability. When self-hosting LDAP in the cloud, administrators must carefully configure security groups, firewall rules, and VPNs or private connectivity options like AWS Direct Connect or Azure ExpressRoute to ensure that directory traffic remains isolated and secure.

LDAP in the cloud brings unique challenges related to security and compliance. In traditional on-premises environments, LDAP servers are typically protected by physical security, firewalls, and segmented networks. In the cloud, however, directory servers are accessible over virtual networks that may span multiple regions and tenants. Encrypting all LDAP communications using SSL/TLS becomes mandatory to prevent credential exposure and to secure data in transit.

LDAP servers should also be integrated with the cloud provider's identity and access management (IAM) services to enforce strong authentication, role-based access controls, and auditing for administrative actions on the directory infrastructure.

Another key aspect of running LDAP in cloud environments is supporting modern identity protocols and integrations. While LDAP remains indispensable for legacy applications and certain internal workflows, many cloud-native applications and services use protocols such as SAML, OAuth2, and OpenID Connect for authentication and authorization. To bridge the gap, organizations often deploy identity federation platforms or identity-as-a-service (IDaaS) solutions that integrate LDAP directories with modern protocols. For example, LDAP user accounts can be synchronized with cloud identity providers, enabling single sign-on to SaaS applications or API services while continuing to use LDAP as the authoritative identity source.

Scaling LDAP services in the cloud requires a shift in thinking from traditional static infrastructure to dynamic, elastic architectures. Cloud-native LDAP deployments can take advantage of features such as auto-scaling to add or remove LDAP replicas based on demand. Load balancers can distribute client queries across multiple LDAP servers deployed in different availability zones, reducing latency and providing redundancy. Replication mechanisms, such as multi-master replication or provider-consumer topologies, ensure that directory data remains synchronized and consistent across all nodes.

LDAP logging and monitoring take on added significance in cloud environments. Administrators must integrate LDAP logs with cloud-native logging and observability tools to gain real-time visibility into service health, security events, and user behaviors. Centralized logging platforms such as AWS CloudWatch, Azure Monitor, or Google Cloud Logging can ingest LDAP logs, while cloud-native metrics services provide dashboards and alerts to track key performance indicators like query latency, bind success rates, and replication status. This visibility is essential for maintaining compliance with regulatory requirements such as GDPR, HIPAA, or PCI DSS, which mandate secure logging and auditing of identity services.

Backup and disaster recovery strategies for cloud-based LDAP services also need to align with cloud best practices. For self-hosted LDAP servers, this includes creating automated snapshots of directory databases, replicating backups across regions, and using cloud provider backup services to ensure quick recovery in the event of data loss or service outages. Managed LDAP services often include built-in backup and restore features, but organizations must still validate recovery processes and ensure that backups are encrypted, tested regularly, and meet retention policy requirements.

In multi-cloud environments, where organizations leverage services from multiple cloud providers, LDAP's role becomes even more complex and critical. LDAP directories may need to integrate with identity platforms in each cloud, requiring synchronization strategies or the use of global identity management platforms that provide a unified view of users and groups across disparate environments. This approach allows organizations to maintain consistent access policies, enforce governance controls, and simplify user provisioning across a diverse cloud landscape.

In addition to its role as a directory service, LDAP in the cloud can be extended to support custom applications and services running within the cloud environment. Developers building cloud-native applications often require centralized user directories for managing application users, enforcing fine-grained access controls, or implementing multi-tenancy models. By leveraging LDAP as a backend, these applications gain a flexible and standards-compliant way to manage identities and integrate with existing enterprise authentication workflows.

LDAP in cloud environments represents a convergence of traditional directory services with the scalability, flexibility, and global reach of modern cloud computing. By thoughtfully designing LDAP deployments that leverage cloud-native capabilities while preserving the security and governance models required by the organization, administrators can ensure that directory services continue to play a foundational role in identity management, application integration, and secure access across hybrid and multi-cloud infrastructures. As organizations increasingly adopt cloud-first strategies, LDAP remains a critical enabler of unified, secure, and scalable identity and access management systems.

LDAP in Hybrid Deployments

LDAP in hybrid deployments plays a crucial role in modern enterprise environments, where organizations operate both on-premises infrastructure and cloud-based services. A hybrid deployment is characterized by the integration of traditional, locally hosted systems with public or private cloud platforms, creating a seamless environment where users and applications can interact regardless of where resources reside. LDAP serves as the foundational directory service that unifies identity management across these disparate environments, enabling consistent authentication, authorization, and user data synchronization between on-premises and cloud components.

One of the primary drivers for adopting LDAP in hybrid deployments is the need for centralized identity and access management across a mixed infrastructure. Many organizations that have historically relied on LDAP-based directories within their on-premises data centers now need to extend those directories to cloud-hosted applications and services. Rather than duplicating identity stores in each environment, a hybrid LDAP deployment allows organizations to maintain a single authoritative source of identity data that supports both on-premises and cloud-based resources. This approach reduces administrative overhead, minimizes identity sprawl, and ensures consistent access controls regardless of where users or applications are located.

In hybrid deployments, LDAP typically operates as the central hub for synchronizing identities with cloud services. For example, an organization may use an on-premises OpenLDAP or Microsoft Active Directory instance as the master directory while synchronizing user accounts, group memberships, and related attributes to cloud-based identity providers such as Azure Active Directory, AWS IAM Identity Center, or Google Cloud Identity. This synchronization allows users to use their corporate LDAP credentials to authenticate to cloud applications through federated identity protocols such as SAML or OpenID Connect while continuing to authenticate to on-premises applications via traditional LDAP binds.

To facilitate synchronization, organizations often deploy directory synchronization tools or identity bridges that connect on-premises LDAP servers to cloud identity platforms. Tools such as Azure AD Connect, Google Cloud Directory Sync, or custom-built solutions automate the process of synchronizing directory objects, reducing the potential for human error and ensuring that user data remains up-to-date across environments. These tools typically include configurable filtering, attribute mapping, and transformation capabilities that allow administrators to control which data is synchronized and how it is represented in the cloud.

LDAP's role in hybrid deployments also extends to supporting legacy applications that remain on-premises. Many enterprise applications, including enterprise resource planning (ERP) systems, intranets, and custom-built business applications, rely on LDAP for user authentication and access control. Maintaining LDAP services within the on-premises environment ensures continued compatibility with these applications, even as other workloads are migrated to the cloud. Meanwhile, new cloud-native applications can integrate with cloud identity providers that are synchronized with the LDAP directory, providing a seamless experience for users.

High availability and redundancy are critical considerations when deploying LDAP in a hybrid model. Since LDAP serves as the central point of identity validation for both environments, its availability directly impacts users' ability to access applications and services. To address this, administrators typically deploy redundant LDAP servers across both on-premises and cloud environments. For example, an organization might maintain LDAP replicas in its primary data center while deploying additional LDAP replicas in the cloud using virtual machines or containerized instances. Load balancers and global traffic managers ensure that client requests are routed to the nearest available LDAP server, reducing latency and providing failover capabilities in case of outages.

Security is paramount in hybrid LDAP deployments due to the increased attack surface created by spanning both private and public infrastructures. All LDAP traffic between on-premises and cloud environments must be encrypted using SSL/TLS to protect against interception and unauthorized access. Administrators must also configure secure network tunnels, such as site-to-site VPNs or dedicated private connectivity like AWS Direct Connect or Azure ExpressRoute, to establish trusted communication channels between the local data center and the cloud. Additionally, service accounts used for synchronization or cross-environment access should follow the principle of least privilege, with permissions restricted to the minimum required for their specific functions.

Hybrid LDAP deployments also require careful attention to schema management and directory design. Schema extensions or custom object classes used in the on-premises LDAP directory may not be fully supported or required in the cloud identity platform. Administrators must ensure schema compatibility and implement attribute transformation rules to map data correctly between systems. Maintaining consistency in naming conventions, group structures, and organizational units is essential for simplifying access control management and ensuring that users experience a coherent directory structure, whether interacting with on-premises or cloud-hosted services.

Identity governance and compliance requirements add another layer of complexity to hybrid LDAP deployments. Organizations must ensure that access to directory data complies with regulations such as GDPR, HIPAA, or SOX, regardless of where the data resides. Logging and auditing mechanisms should capture events from both on-premises and cloud-based LDAP servers and identity platforms, providing a unified view of authentication attempts, directory changes, and administrative actions across the hybrid environment. Centralized SIEM solutions and log aggregation platforms help organizations correlate security events and maintain visibility across distributed systems.

Performance optimization is also critical for hybrid LDAP deployments, as directory queries may originate from applications and users located in different parts of the world. Deploying LDAP replicas closer to cloud-hosted services or remote offices can significantly reduce query latency and improve the user experience. Caching mechanisms, such as LDAP proxy servers or client-side caches, can further enhance performance by reducing the frequency of queries sent to the central directory.

In addition to supporting traditional LDAP workflows, hybrid deployments enable organizations to adopt modern identity models such as single sign-on (SSO) and multi-factor authentication (MFA) more easily. Cloud identity providers synchronized with LDAP directories can integrate with a wide range of SSO-enabled applications, providing users with seamless access to SaaS platforms, cloud-native services, and APIs. At the same time, organizations can enforce stronger authentication policies, such as requiring MFA for access to sensitive resources, while maintaining centralized identity data in LDAP.

As organizations continue to embrace digital transformation and expand their use of cloud services, LDAP's role in hybrid deployments remains indispensable. The ability to bridge on-premises and cloud environments with a unified identity store allows enterprises to modernize their IT infrastructure while preserving investments in legacy systems and applications. By carefully planning LDAP architectures, synchronization strategies, and security controls, organizations can create robust hybrid deployments that deliver secure, efficient, and seamless identity management across all layers of their technology stack.

LDAP and DevOps Workflows

LDAP and DevOps workflows intersect in several critical areas where automation, consistency, and security are key priorities. DevOps practices emphasize the rapid deployment, scaling, and management of applications and infrastructure through continuous integration and continuous delivery (CI/CD) pipelines, Infrastructure as Code (IaC), and automated testing. In this context, LDAP plays a pivotal role as a centralized identity and access management system, enabling streamlined authentication, authorization, and configuration management processes that align with DevOps principles. Integrating LDAP into DevOps workflows helps organizations automate identity-related tasks, maintain compliance, and ensure secure access to services and infrastructure.

One of the primary ways LDAP is leveraged in DevOps workflows is through automated user and service account management. In traditional IT environments, provisioning and deprovisioning users in the directory might be manual, time-consuming tasks prone to errors and inconsistencies. However, in DevOps, these operations are increasingly automated using scripts, APIs, and orchestration tools that interact with LDAP servers. For example, onboarding processes for new employees or developers can be integrated into CI/CD pipelines, where a new LDAP entry is automatically created as part of a user creation workflow. By defining user provisioning as code, administrators ensure that every user is configured consistently, with the correct roles, group memberships, and access rights based on predefined templates or policies.

LDAP's integration into Infrastructure as Code is also common in DevOps environments. Configuration management tools such as Ansible, Puppet, and Chef include LDAP modules or plugins that allow administrators to manage directory entries, modify ACLs, or configure LDAP-based authentication for servers and services as part of automated deployment routines. For instance, an Ansible playbook may configure a fleet of Linux servers to authenticate users against an LDAP directory, enforce sudo policies based on LDAP groups, and ensure that all relevant LDAP settings are applied uniformly across all nodes in the environment. This eliminates configuration drift, improves security, and supports repeatable and auditable deployments.

In containerized and microservices-based architectures, LDAP can be integrated with container orchestration platforms like Kubernetes to manage identity and access controls. Kubernetes clusters may rely on LDAP to authenticate administrative users or service accounts that interact with the Kubernetes API. By tying Kubernetes Role-Based Access Control (RBAC) to LDAP groups, DevOps teams can centralize access management and simplify permissions assignments. Automation tools such as Helm or Kustomize can be used to package LDAP integration configurations into deployment templates, ensuring that new clusters and services are consistently configured to leverage LDAP authentication.

LDAP also enhances CI/CD pipelines by providing secure, centralized authentication for DevOps tools and platforms. Continuous integration servers like Jenkins or GitLab CI can be configured to authenticate users via LDAP, enforcing role-based access controls within these tools based on group memberships in the directory. This streamlines user management across the DevOps toolchain and ensures that permissions are enforced consistently across the entire CI/CD lifecycle. Automation scripts running in pipelines can also query LDAP directories to retrieve user metadata, populate configuration files, or trigger access control checks as part of deployment and testing stages.

Service accounts, which are widely used in DevOps to enable automated processes to interact with systems and APIs, can also be managed through LDAP. Defining service accounts as LDAP entries allows DevOps teams to control these accounts using the same access policies and security standards applied to human users. Service accounts can be assigned to specific organizational units (OUs) or LDAP groups, making it easier to apply ACLs, audit usage, and rotate credentials programmatically. By automating the creation, modification, and revocation of service accounts through CI/CD pipelines or configuration management tools, organizations can reduce manual intervention and strengthen the security posture of their DevOps workflows.

Security and compliance are key concerns in DevOps environments, especially when deploying services at scale. LDAP helps address these concerns by enabling centralized auditing and logging of authentication and authorization events. By integrating LDAP logs into centralized log aggregation or SIEM systems, DevOps teams gain visibility into access patterns and can quickly detect anomalies, such as unauthorized access attempts or privilege escalations. Automated alerting can be configured to notify security teams of suspicious activities related to DevOps pipelines, infrastructure, or applications that authenticate via LDAP.

Secrets management is another area where LDAP contributes to DevOps workflows. While tools like HashiCorp Vault, AWS Secrets Manager, or Azure Key Vault are often used to manage secrets, LDAP directories can serve as an identity provider for these platforms, enforcing authentication and access control based on LDAP-defined policies. For example, developers accessing Vault may authenticate using their LDAP credentials, and Vault policies may be mapped to LDAP groups to determine which secrets users or services are permitted to retrieve. This centralization helps maintain a secure and auditable secrets management workflow while integrating smoothly into the broader DevOps ecosystem.

LDAP also supports automation around compliance and governance within DevOps workflows. Compliance frameworks often require that access to critical systems is controlled, auditable, and based on formalized approval processes. DevOps teams can automate access request workflows that interact with LDAP, ensuring that new permissions or group memberships are only applied after the necessary approvals are obtained. These workflows can be implemented through ticketing systems, CI/CD pipelines, or identity governance platforms that integrate with LDAP to enforce segregation of duties and reduce the risk of non-compliant actions.

Testing and validation are integral to DevOps pipelines, and LDAP can be part of this process. Automated testing frameworks may include LDAP-backed test scenarios where pipelines validate that applications can successfully authenticate against the directory, retrieve user attributes, or respect role-based access controls. Test environments can be provisioned with temporary LDAP directories containing predefined test users and groups, enabling end-to-end testing of authentication and authorization flows before code is promoted to production.

In large-scale DevOps environments, LDAP also facilitates cross-team collaboration by simplifying access management. Development, operations, security, and QA teams can all authenticate to shared platforms using LDAP accounts, while group memberships dictate what level of access each team member has. This fosters a culture of shared responsibility while maintaining appropriate separation of duties across the DevOps lifecycle.

The integration of LDAP into DevOps workflows not only strengthens identity and access management but also enhances automation, reduces operational overhead, and ensures that security and compliance are embedded into every phase of the software delivery pipeline. By leveraging LDAP's capabilities as part of their DevOps toolchain, organizations can build scalable, secure, and efficient workflows that align with modern development and operations practices.

Scripting LDAP Operations

Scripting LDAP operations is a powerful technique that enables administrators to automate routine directory management tasks, streamline identity workflows, and integrate LDAP functionality into broader IT automation processes. While graphical user interfaces and LDAP administration tools provide convenient ways to interact with directory services, scripting allows for greater flexibility, repeatability, and scalability, particularly in large environments where thousands of directory objects must be managed efficiently. By writing scripts, administrators can automate tasks such as adding and deleting entries, modifying attributes, managing group memberships, performing searches, and integrating LDAP operations into DevOps pipelines or provisioning systems.

One of the most common scripting environments for LDAP operations is the shell, where administrators use command-line tools such as ldapsearch, ldapadd, ldapmodify, and ldapdelete. These utilities are standard in most LDAP distributions and provide basic functionality for interacting with the directory over the LDAP protocol. For example, a simple shell script using ldapadd can automate the bulk creation of user accounts by reading an LDIF file that contains multiple user entries. By combining ldapadd with loop constructs and input validation, administrators can create scripts that generate LDIF entries dynamically based on external data sources such as CSV files, SQL databases, or RESTful APIs.

ldapsearch is a versatile tool for querying directory data within scripts. It can be used to extract user details, group memberships, or other directory objects and pipe the results into other scripts for further processing. For instance, a shell script might use ldapsearch to retrieve a list of users in a specific organizational unit and then pass the results to another script that updates user attributes or generates audit reports. LDAP search filters can be incorporated directly into scripts, allowing precise control over which entries are targeted based on attributes such as objectClass, uid, or group membership.

Beyond shell scripting, many administrators and developers leverage programming languages such as Python, Perl, or PowerShell to script LDAP operations. Python, for example, offers the python-ldap library, which provides a rich set of functions for performing LDAP binds, searches, modifications, and deletions. Using python-ldap, a script can establish a connection to an LDAP server, authenticate using service account credentials, and execute complex queries or updates programmatically. Python's flexibility also makes it ideal for integrating LDAP with other services, such as sending notifications when directory changes occur, interacting with APIs, or automating user onboarding workflows that involve multiple systems.

An example Python script might query an LDAP directory for inactive accounts and then automatically disable them by modifying the user account status attribute. The script could also log each modification for auditing purposes and send an email summary to system administrators. This level of automation is particularly valuable for maintaining directory hygiene and ensuring compliance with organizational policies regarding inactive or orphaned accounts.

PowerShell is another popular choice for scripting LDAP operations, especially in environments that use Microsoft Active Directory. PowerShell's native Active Directory module includes cmdlets such as Get-ADUser, Set-ADUser, and Remove-ADUser, which simplify the process of managing directory objects in Windows-based environments. PowerShell scripts can perform bulk operations, such as resetting passwords for a list of users or updating user attributes based on external data feeds. These scripts can be scheduled to run automatically or integrated into broader automation platforms like System Center Orchestrator or Azure Automation.

Scripting LDAP operations also enables the automation of group membership management. For example, a script can periodically synchronize group memberships with external data sources, ensuring that users are assigned to the correct LDAP groups based on their department, job role, or project assignment. This dynamic approach reduces manual intervention, keeps access control lists accurate, and supports role-based access control policies across the organization.

In addition to administrative tasks, scripts can also be used to enforce directory policies. A script might search for directory entries that violate schema rules or naming conventions and generate alerts or corrective actions. For example, a compliance script could detect user accounts missing mandatory attributes like email addresses or phone numbers and automatically notify administrators for remediation. Similarly, scripts can enforce password policies by identifying accounts with weak or non-compliant passwords and prompting users to reset them.

Scripting is often combined with version control systems like Git to manage and track changes to LDAP automation scripts. By maintaining scripts in repositories, administrators can collaborate on LDAP automation projects, review changes through pull requests, and deploy scripts using CI/CD pipelines. This approach aligns with Infrastructure as Code practices and ensures that LDAP management workflows are consistent, reproducible, and subject to change management processes.

Error handling and logging are important considerations when scripting LDAP operations. Scripts should include logic to capture and handle common LDAP errors, such as authentication failures, schema violations, or insufficient access rights. Detailed logs should record the results of each operation, including timestamps, affected entries, and any encountered errors. This information is invaluable for troubleshooting and auditing, particularly when running scripts in production environments.

Security is a key concern when automating LDAP tasks. Scripts that perform LDAP operations often require service account credentials, which must be stored securely. Administrators should avoid hardcoding passwords directly into scripts and instead use secure credential storage mechanisms such as environment variables, encrypted vaults, or secret management services. Additionally, service accounts used by scripts should follow the principle of least privilege, with permissions limited to only the necessary directory objects and operations.

LDAP automation scripts can also play a role in disaster recovery and backup workflows. For instance, scripts can be scheduled to export LDAP directory data to LDIF files at regular intervals, providing point-in-time backups of directory entries. In the event of data loss or corruption, corresponding restore scripts can automate the re-import of LDIF data into the directory, minimizing downtime and manual recovery efforts.

Scripting LDAP operations enhances the efficiency, consistency, and security of directory management. It enables administrators to scale their efforts across large environments, reduce repetitive tasks, and integrate LDAP into modern DevOps and IT automation workflows. By mastering scripting techniques, LDAP administrators can transform complex directory operations into streamlined processes that improve operational agility and support the evolving identity and access management needs of their organizations.

Automating LDAP with Python

Automating LDAP with Python provides administrators and developers with a highly flexible and efficient way to manage directory services and streamline identity-related workflows. LDAP, as a protocol, is essential in many organizations for managing user accounts, group memberships, and access control policies across a range of systems and applications. By leveraging Python's powerful libraries and scripting capabilities, organizations can automate common LDAP tasks such as querying directory data, modifying user records, provisioning new accounts, and integrating LDAP operations into broader automation pipelines.

One of the key advantages of using Python for LDAP automation is the availability of the python-ldap library, a well-established module that provides a Python interface to LDAP directory servers. This library enables Python scripts to establish connections to LDAP servers, perform bind operations for authentication, and execute a full range of

LDAP commands, including search, add, modify, and delete operations. The python-ldap library abstracts the complexities of the LDAP protocol, offering high-level functions and data structures that simplify directory interaction.

The process of automating LDAP with Python typically begins by initializing a connection to the directory server. A Python script can use python-ldap to create a connection object, specify the LDAP server URI, and perform a bind operation using a service account or administrative credentials. The script can then reuse this connection to perform multiple LDAP operations without re-authenticating, making it suitable for bulk tasks such as provisioning hundreds of user accounts or processing large-scale updates.

For example, a Python script might automate the onboarding process for new employees by reading data from a CSV file or human resources database, generating LDAP entries based on predefined templates, and adding these entries to the directory. Each user entry can be constructed as a Python dictionary that maps attribute names to their respective values, such as cn, sn, mail, and userPassword. The script then uses the add_s() method from python-ldap to insert the new entries into the directory. This automation eliminates the need for manual data entry, reduces the likelihood of human error, and ensures that new accounts are provisioned with the correct attributes and access levels.

Python is also well-suited for automating LDAP search operations, which are essential for tasks such as generating reports, auditing directory data, or integrating LDAP with other applications. A Python script can use the search_s() method to perform queries against the directory based on filters such as (objectClass=person) or (memberOf=cn=admins,ou=groups,dc=example,dc=com). The search results are returned as a list of tuples containing distinguished names and attribute dictionaries, which can be processed to extract relevant information, create audit logs, or trigger further automated actions. For example, a script might search for inactive accounts based on the last login timestamp and automatically disable them or send notifications to administrators for review.

Modifying existing entries is another common LDAP automation use case for Python. A script can use the modify_s() method to apply changes to attributes, such as updating a user's email address, changing group memberships, or resetting a password. Python's control flow capabilities allow for conditional logic, enabling the script to apply updates only when specific criteria are met. For instance, a script might iterate through user accounts and update the department attribute only for users whose job roles have changed, as indicated by data from an external HR system.

Python's versatility also makes it ideal for automating LDAP operations as part of DevOps workflows. For example, Python scripts can be integrated into CI/CD pipelines to manage service accounts, provision resources, or configure authentication settings for newly deployed applications. These scripts can automate the creation of organizational units, the assignment of service accounts to specific LDAP groups, and the enforcement of access control policies, all of which are critical tasks in cloud-native and containerized environments. By embedding LDAP automation directly into deployment workflows, organizations can reduce deployment times, increase consistency, and ensure that infrastructure components are securely integrated with the directory service.

Error handling is an important aspect of LDAP automation with Python. The python-ldap library raises exceptions for common LDAP errors, such as invalid credentials, schema violations, or insufficient access rights. Scripts should include robust exception handling to capture and log these errors, provide meaningful messages for troubleshooting, and implement fallback procedures where appropriate. For example, if a script encounters an LDAP error when attempting to modify an entry, it can automatically retry the operation, alert an administrator, or roll back related changes to maintain data integrity.

Security considerations are critical when automating LDAP operations. Scripts often require service account credentials to bind to the LDAP server, and these credentials should be protected using secure storage mechanisms such as environment variables, encrypted configuration files, or secret management services like HashiCorp Vault. Additionally, all LDAP connections should be secured using SSL/TLS to protect directory traffic from eavesdropping or tampering. Python's ssl module can be used in conjunction with python-ldap to enforce secure connections and validate server certificates as part of the script's connection logic.

Automation with Python also enables LDAP integration with other enterprise systems. Python scripts can combine LDAP queries with REST API calls, database queries, or cloud service integrations to create end-to-end automation workflows. For instance, a script might query LDAP for a list of users in a specific group and then use an API to provision access to a SaaS application based on those group memberships. Similarly, Python automation can be used to synchronize LDAP data with cloud identity providers, automate ticket creation in IT service management platforms, or send notifications through messaging systems such as Slack or Microsoft Teams.

Python's data processing capabilities further enhance LDAP automation. Scripts can manipulate data retrieved from the directory, such as generating formatted reports, aggregating statistics, or applying business logic to directory records. For example, a reporting script might extract user data from LDAP, calculate statistics on group sizes or organizational structures, and generate CSV or PDF reports for compliance and auditing purposes. This automated approach reduces manual effort and ensures that reporting tasks are performed consistently and accurately.

Automating LDAP with Python provides organizations with a powerful set of tools to simplify directory management, improve operational efficiency, and support secure and scalable identity workflows. Whether used for provisioning, maintenance, reporting, or integration tasks, Python-based LDAP automation empowers administrators and developers to build robust solutions that align with modern IT practices and the increasing demand for agility and automation in today's complex enterprise environments.

LDAP Integration with Web Applications

LDAP integration with web applications is a cornerstone of centralized identity and access management strategies within modern organizations. Web applications often require robust user authentication mechanisms to ensure that only authorized users can access specific resources or perform certain operations. By integrating web applications with LDAP directories, organizations can centralize authentication, streamline user management, and enforce consistent security policies across a variety of platforms. LDAP provides a scalable and standardized way to authenticate users and retrieve user information, making it an ideal backend for web applications operating in both on-premises and cloud environments.

The most fundamental aspect of LDAP integration with web applications is user authentication. Instead of maintaining local databases of user credentials within each web application, developers can configure their applications to authenticate against a central LDAP directory. This approach eliminates the redundancy of managing multiple sets of credentials and reduces administrative overhead, as user accounts and passwords are managed in one place. When a user logs into a web application, the application typically performs an LDAP bind operation using the user's provided credentials. If the bind is successful, the user is authenticated and granted access based on the application's internal authorization logic.

The typical authentication flow in an LDAP-integrated web application involves a two-step process. First, the application performs an LDAP search to locate the distinguished name of the user based on a unique identifier such as the username or email address. Common LDAP attributes used in this search include uid, cn, or mail, depending on the schema in place. Once the distinguished name is retrieved, the application attempts to bind to the LDAP server using the distinguished name and the password provided by the user. A successful bind indicates that the credentials are valid, allowing the application to create a session and grant access.

Beyond authentication, LDAP integration allows web applications to retrieve additional user attributes, such as full name, email address, department, or group memberships. These attributes can be used to personalize the user interface, populate user profiles, or determine role-based permissions within the application. For example, a user who is a member of the cn=admins,ou=groups,dc=example,dc=com group in LDAP might be granted administrative privileges within the web application, while other users may only have standard access. This mapping of LDAP groups to application roles streamlines access management and ensures that permissions are consistent across all systems integrated with the directory.

Most modern web application frameworks and content management systems provide native support or third-party modules for LDAP integration. For example, popular platforms like Drupal, WordPress, and Joomla offer plugins that allow administrators to configure LDAP authentication without writing custom code. Similarly, enterprise-grade applications such as Atlassian Jira, Confluence, and GitLab include built-in LDAP connectors that can be easily configured to interact with LDAP servers for user management. These connectors typically allow administrators to specify connection parameters, search bases, filters, and attribute mappings through a graphical user interface, simplifying the integration process.

For custom web applications, developers often rely on LDAP client libraries provided for programming languages such as Python, PHP, Java, or Node.js. These libraries abstract the low-level LDAP protocol details and provide high-level functions for performing binds, searches, and modifications. For instance, a Java web application might use the JNDI API to interact with LDAP, while a Python-based web service could leverage the python-ldap library. By incorporating LDAP operations directly into the application's authentication layer, developers can build seamless integrations that support single sign-on and centralized user management.

Security is a critical consideration when integrating web applications with LDAP. All communication between the web application and the LDAP server should be encrypted using SSL/TLS to protect credentials and sensitive directory data from interception. Most LDAP servers support LDAPS on port 636 or StartTLS on port 389, and web applications should be configured to enforce secure connections during LDAP interactions. Additionally, the service account used by the web application to perform LDAP searches should follow the principle of least privilege, with read-only permissions restricted to the relevant organizational units and attributes required for authentication and user profile lookups.

To further enhance security, many organizations integrate LDAP-backed web applications with centralized single sign-on (SSO) solutions. SSO platforms act as intermediaries that authenticate users against the LDAP directory and issue tokens or assertions to web applications using protocols such as SAML, OAuth2, or OpenID Connect. This approach reduces password fatigue by allowing users to log in once and gain access to multiple web applications without re-entering credentials. It also centralizes authentication policies such as password complexity, expiration, and multi-factor authentication, improving the overall security posture.

Load balancing and high availability should also be factored into LDAP integration with web applications. In environments with multiple LDAP servers or replicas, web applications can be configured to query multiple servers for failover and redundancy. Most LDAP client libraries and connectors support connection failover logic or allow administrators to specify multiple server addresses. This ensures that web applications remain operational even if one LDAP server becomes unavailable. Load balancers placed in front of LDAP servers can also distribute traffic evenly across the infrastructure, enhancing performance and resilience.

Performance tuning is essential, especially in high-traffic web applications. Developers should ensure that LDAP queries are optimized by using appropriate search filters, limiting search scopes to relevant organizational units, and retrieving only the necessary attributes. Additionally, LDAP servers should be configured with indexes on frequently queried attributes to reduce query processing times. Some web applications implement caching mechanisms to store LDAP query results temporarily, reducing the number of LDAP operations required for recurring sessions and improving overall responsiveness.

Logging and monitoring are crucial to maintaining visibility into LDAP-integrated web applications. Web applications should log LDAP authentication events, including successful and failed login attempts, search queries, and errors encountered during directory operations. These logs provide valuable insights for troubleshooting authentication issues and detecting security incidents such as brute-force attacks or suspicious login patterns. Integration with centralized logging and monitoring platforms allows security teams to correlate LDAP events with other infrastructure logs, supporting proactive incident response and audit compliance.

LDAP integration with web applications also supports user self-service features. For example, applications can offer password reset functionality by leveraging LDAP password modification operations, provided that the directory supports password changes via standard LDAP modify requests. Other self-service features, such as profile updates or group membership requests, can also be facilitated by interacting with LDAP to apply the necessary modifications. Automating these workflows through LDAP integration enhances user experience while reducing the administrative burden on IT teams.

In large-scale deployments, LDAP integration with web applications extends to hybrid and multi-cloud environments. Web applications hosted in public cloud platforms or in geographically distributed data centers can authenticate users against centralized LDAP directories using VPN tunnels, direct cloud interconnects, or cloud-native LDAP services. This capability supports organizations that operate global web services and require consistent identity management across multiple regions or cloud providers.

Integrating LDAP with web applications enables organizations to centralize identity management, improve security, and simplify user administration. Whether through native connectors, custom code, or SSO integrations, LDAP provides a flexible and reliable foundation for authenticating users and enforcing access controls across a diverse ecosystem of web-based platforms and services. As web applications continue to serve as the interface for critical business processes, LDAP remains a fundamental component in securing and streamlining user access.

LDAP and Microservices Architectures

LDAP and microservices architectures intersect at a critical point where identity and access management must be unified across highly distributed and modular systems. In a microservices architecture, applications are decomposed into small, independent services that each handle specific business functions. These services communicate with one another via APIs and are often deployed independently, scaling as needed based on application demands. While microservices provide advantages in terms of scalability, flexibility, and faster development cycles, they also introduce complexities in managing authentication, authorization, and user data across multiple services. LDAP plays a key role in providing a centralized identity service that microservices can rely on to standardize and secure identity workflows across the ecosystem.

In a monolithic application, authentication and user management may be handled by a single component or module. However, in a microservices model, multiple services often require knowledge of user identities and access privileges. Rather than duplicating identity stores across each microservice, organizations use LDAP as a centralized directory that all services can query to authenticate users, validate permissions, and retrieve profile information. By externalizing identity management to LDAP, developers can decouple authentication logic from individual microservices, promoting code reusability and reducing maintenance overhead.

One of the most common ways LDAP is integrated into microservices architectures is by positioning it as a backend for an identity provider or authentication gateway. Instead of having each microservice communicate directly with the LDAP server, a centralized authentication service or API gateway is implemented. This gateway acts as the primary interface between external clients and the microservices layer, handling user login requests, performing LDAP authentication, and issuing tokens such as JWTs (JSON Web Tokens) to authenticated clients. These tokens can then be passed to individual microservices as proof of identity, allowing services to validate the token locally without querying LDAP directly for each request.

This token-based approach improves performance and reduces the load on the LDAP server, which might otherwise be overwhelmed by high volumes of authentication queries from multiple microservices. Once a user has authenticated successfully through the gateway, subsequent requests to the microservices simply include the token, which can be validated using a shared secret or public key. This model not only simplifies communication between microservices but also allows for stateless service design, which is a fundamental principle of microservices architecture.

LDAP's group and role management capabilities are also leveraged extensively in microservices environments. Organizations often map LDAP groups to specific roles or permissions within the microservices ecosystem. For instance, users belonging to the cn=developers,ou=groups,dc=example,dc=com LDAP group may be granted access to development-related APIs or services, while those in cn=admins may receive elevated privileges. The authentication gateway or identity provider is responsible for embedding group or role information into the token payload, allowing microservices to enforce fine-grained access controls based on claims in the token. This centralized approach to authorization simplifies policy management and ensures that permissions are consistent across all services.

LDAP also supports service-to-service authentication within microservices architectures. In scenarios where microservices need to authenticate to each other or to external systems, LDAP directories can be used to manage service accounts or machine identities. These accounts are defined as LDAP entries with appropriate credentials and access policies. By storing service accounts in LDAP, administrators can enforce password rotation policies, audit service authentication events, and apply access control policies centrally.

Microservices are often deployed in dynamic, containerized environments orchestrated by platforms such as Kubernetes. In such environments, LDAP can integrate with Kubernetes RBAC (Role-Based Access Control) mechanisms to manage cluster access. Developers and operations personnel authenticate to the Kubernetes API via LDAP credentials, with group memberships determining their permissions within the cluster. Similarly, Kubernetes-native tools such as ingress controllers or service meshes like Istio can integrate with centralized

LDAP-backed identity providers to enforce authentication and authorization at the network layer.

LDAP's extensibility is advantageous in microservices ecosystems where diverse services may require different sets of user attributes. LDAP schemas can be customized to include additional attributes relevant to microservices, such as API access tokens, custom roles, or service-level agreements (SLAs) associated with a user. These attributes can then be retrieved during the authentication process and passed to microservices as part of token claims or API headers, supporting business-specific authorization logic.

Monitoring and auditing LDAP interactions within a microservices architecture is critical for security and compliance. Centralized logging solutions capture authentication events, including successful and failed login attempts, changes to group memberships, and access control violations. These logs provide visibility into user activity across the entire ecosystem, enabling organizations to detect anomalies, investigate incidents, and meet compliance requirements. Integrating LDAP logs with SIEM platforms ensures that identity-related events are correlated with application and infrastructure logs, providing a holistic view of security across the distributed system.

Security is further strengthened by enforcing encryption and secure channels for all LDAP communications. Microservices and authentication gateways should use LDAPS or StartTLS to protect user credentials and directory data during transmission. LDAP servers should implement strict access control policies to ensure that only trusted components, such as the authentication gateway or specific services, can perform directory queries or modifications.

The automation of LDAP integration into microservices pipelines is another key benefit. DevOps workflows can leverage configuration management tools like Ansible or Terraform to provision LDAP service accounts, configure access controls, and deploy authentication services alongside microservices. CI/CD pipelines can include stages that automatically synchronize LDAP configurations with the latest application releases, ensuring that identity and access management remains aligned with evolving application requirements.

In complex microservices ecosystems, where services span multiple cloud providers or hybrid environments, LDAP plays a unifying role by providing a centralized directory that supports consistent identity management across all deployment platforms. LDAP's ability to integrate with hybrid and multi-cloud environments ensures that users and services maintain a single identity across geographically distributed and heterogeneous infrastructures.

LDAP's role in microservices architectures ensures that organizations can scale identity management alongside their application ecosystems. By centralizing authentication and authorization through LDAP, organizations gain the benefits of streamlined user management, reduced complexity within services, and improved security across all layers of the architecture. As microservices continue to proliferate as the standard architectural model for modern applications, LDAP's flexibility and scalability make it a critical component of secure and efficient identity and access management strategies.

Advanced LDAP Schema Design

Advanced LDAP schema design is a critical component of building scalable, efficient, and flexible directory services. The schema defines the structure and rules governing how data is stored in an LDAP directory, including object classes, attributes, syntaxes, and matching rules. While default schemas provided by LDAP servers such as OpenLDAP or Microsoft Active Directory offer a broad set of common object classes and attributes, many organizations require schema extensions to meet their unique business and technical needs. Crafting a robust and extensible schema is essential to ensure data integrity, optimize directory performance, and support evolving application requirements.

An LDAP schema consists of object classes that define the types of entries that can be stored in the directory and attributes that specify the data fields for those entries. Object classes are categorized as structural, auxiliary, or abstract. Structural object classes define the core type of an entry and must be present in every entry. Auxiliary object classes can be added to existing entries to provide additional

149

attributes, while abstract object classes serve as templates from which structural classes inherit attributes. Designing an advanced schema often involves creating custom structural and auxiliary object classes that model the organization's specific entities, such as employees, contractors, devices, or applications.

When designing custom object classes, administrators must consider both the mandatory and optional attributes that each class will include. Mandatory attributes, also known as MUST attributes, are required for an entry to conform to the schema, while optional attributes, known as MAY attributes, provide additional flexibility. For example, a custom object class for external consultants might mandate attributes such as cn (common name), uid (user ID), and mail (email address), while allowing optional fields like phoneNumber or projectCode. The careful selection of attributes ensures that entries have sufficient information for directory operations while avoiding unnecessary complexity.

Advanced schema design also involves extending or reusing existing object classes to promote compatibility with widely adopted standards. Many applications and services expect directory entries to conform to standard schemas, such as inetOrgPerson, which is commonly used for user entries. By extending standard object classes with auxiliary classes or additional attributes, organizations can enhance functionality without sacrificing interoperability. For instance, an organization may create an auxiliary object class that adds attributes like employeeStatus or contractEndDate to the inetOrgPerson structural class, allowing for better representation of workforce metadata.

Attribute definition is another key aspect of advanced schema design. Each attribute must have a unique object identifier (OID), a name, a syntax, and matching rules. The syntax determines the format of the attribute's value, such as directory string, integer, or binary data. Matching rules define how attribute values are compared during search operations. For example, attributes like email addresses may use case-insensitive matching rules, while numeric attributes might require equality or ordering matching. Properly defining attribute syntaxes and matching rules improves query accuracy and performance, as LDAP servers can apply optimized indexing and search algorithms.

Naming conventions play a critical role in schema design by maintaining clarity and preventing conflicts. It is common practice to namespace custom object classes and attributes using the organization's domain or a unique prefix. For example, a company with the domain example.com might define a custom attribute as exampleDepartmentCode or exEmployeeType to distinguish it from standard schema elements. Consistent naming conventions also simplify schema maintenance and documentation, making it easier for administrators and developers to understand and extend the schema over time.

Schema design must account for data normalization to ensure consistency and reliability across directory entries. For instance, attributes that store country codes, department names, or job titles should use controlled vocabularies or standardized formats. This practice reduces discrepancies and facilitates integration with external systems that rely on predictable attribute values. Additionally, implementing validation rules through client-side applications or provisioning workflows helps enforce data quality standards at the point of entry.

Performance considerations are integral to advanced schema design. Attributes that are frequently queried or used in search filters should be indexed appropriately to accelerate lookup times. Administrators must balance indexing needs with storage and processing overhead, as excessive indexing can degrade write performance and increase memory consumption. Advanced schema designs often involve analyzing query patterns and user behavior to identify the most critical attributes for indexing, such as uid, mail, or memberOf.

Another important element of schema design is planning for scalability and future growth. As organizations expand or evolve their IT landscapes, directory requirements may change to accommodate new entities, services, or regulatory demands. A well-designed schema anticipates such changes by supporting modular extensions and minimizing rigid dependencies between object classes. For example, instead of embedding all attributes into a single complex object class, designers can create modular auxiliary classes that can be attached to entries as needed, facilitating incremental schema updates without disruptive reengineering.

Schema replication is a consideration in distributed LDAP environments. In multi-master or provider-consumer replication setups, schema consistency must be maintained across all LDAP servers to prevent replication conflicts or operational failures. Administrators should implement schema change management processes, including version control, peer reviews, and controlled deployment pipelines, to ensure that schema updates are thoroughly tested and uniformly applied to all directory nodes.

Security also plays a crucial role in advanced schema design. Sensitive attributes, such as userPassword or socialSecurityNumber, should be protected by applying fine-grained access control lists (ACLs) that restrict read, write, or search permissions based on user roles. By segmenting attributes into different object classes or utilizing auxiliary classes for sensitive data, administrators can more easily apply targeted security policies. Additionally, attributes that store sensitive information should adhere to encryption and data protection requirements specified by industry regulations or internal security policies.

In highly integrated environments, LDAP schema design may need to accommodate external systems that rely on directory data for provisioning, authentication, or reporting purposes. For example, identity governance platforms, HR systems, or customer relationship management (CRM) tools may synchronize with LDAP directories to extract user data or enforce compliance workflows. Schema designers must ensure that attributes required by these systems are present and consistently populated, facilitating smooth integration and reducing the need for data transformations or middleware.

Advanced LDAP schema design is as much an art as it is a technical exercise. It requires a deep understanding of the organization's identity management needs, the structure of its IT ecosystem, and the operational requirements of the applications and services that will interact with the directory. A well-crafted schema not only improves directory efficiency and scalability but also serves as the foundation for secure, consistent, and future-proof identity management practices across the enterprise. By balancing flexibility with standardization and performance with extensibility, advanced schema design empowers organizations to unlock the full potential of their LDAP infrastructure.

LDAP Change Notifications

LDAP change notifications play a vital role in modern directory services by providing real-time updates when directory data is modified. These notifications are essential for synchronizing LDAP directories with other systems, triggering automated workflows, and maintaining data consistency across applications and services that rely on directory information. Rather than relying solely on scheduled polling or periodic synchronization, LDAP change notification mechanisms enable external systems to respond immediately to modifications such as user account updates, password changes, group membership alterations, or the creation and deletion of entries. Implementing change notifications enhances the responsiveness and efficiency of identity and access management processes.

The standard LDAP protocol includes several mechanisms for supporting change notifications, with Persistent Search and the LDAP Content Synchronization (RFC 4533) being two of the most common approaches. Persistent Search, introduced as an LDAP control, allows clients to maintain an open connection to the directory server and receive notifications about changes that match specific search criteria. When an LDAP entry is added, modified, or deleted, the server sends a notification to the client containing the relevant change data. This model is useful for applications that require near-instant updates, such as identity governance platforms, provisioning tools, or audit and compliance systems.

LDAP Content Synchronization, also known as syncrepl in OpenLDAP environments, is a more advanced and standardized mechanism that provides both initial data synchronization and ongoing change notifications. With syncrepl, an LDAP client first performs a full synchronization to retrieve the current state of a directory subtree and then establishes a persistent session to receive incremental updates as changes occur. Each change is assigned a unique synchronization cookie or identifier, allowing the client to track which updates have been processed and resume synchronization seamlessly in the event of a connection loss. This model is widely used in LDAP replication topologies but can also be applied to external applications that require real-time awareness of directory changes.

Implementing change notifications typically involves configuring the LDAP server to support persistent search or syncrepl controls and ensuring that client applications are capable of handling incoming change messages. For example, a provisioning system integrated with LDAP might listen for change notifications on user entries within a specific organizational unit and automatically propagate those updates to downstream applications such as enterprise resource planning (ERP) platforms, SaaS services, or customer relationship management (CRM) systems. This integration minimizes data discrepancies and ensures that identity-related changes are reflected consistently across the enterprise.

Change notifications are particularly valuable in environments where rapid response times are critical. For instance, if an employee's role changes and their LDAP group membership is updated to grant additional access rights, the associated change notification can trigger an immediate update to access control lists in other systems, ensuring that the employee gains the required permissions without delay. Similarly, when a user is terminated and their LDAP account is disabled or deleted, connected systems can promptly revoke access, reducing the risk of unauthorized actions by former employees.

LDAP change notifications also enhance security monitoring and compliance by enabling real-time alerting and audit capabilities. Security Information and Event Management (SIEM) platforms can subscribe to LDAP change events and correlate them with logs from other systems to detect anomalies or unauthorized activities. For example, an alert can be generated if a privileged account's attributes are modified outside of an approved change window, or if sensitive group memberships are altered unexpectedly. Integrating LDAP change notifications with security automation tools can further streamline incident response processes, triggering automated remediation actions such as disabling compromised accounts or enforcing step-up authentication.

To handle LDAP change notifications effectively, applications must be designed to process and interpret the change data provided by the server. Notifications typically include the distinguished name of the affected entry, the type of change (add, modify, delete), and a list of attributes that were modified along with their new values. Some LDAP servers also provide extended information such as modification timestamps or operational attributes indicating the user who performed the change. Consuming applications must implement logic to process these updates accurately, handle potential conflicts, and maintain data integrity across integrated systems.

Performance considerations are important when implementing change notification mechanisms. Maintaining persistent connections for notifications can increase the load on LDAP servers, especially in environments with high transaction volumes or a large number of subscribed clients. Administrators should carefully plan the deployment of change notification consumers to avoid overwhelming the directory infrastructure. Load balancing, connection pooling, and selective filtering based on search criteria can help mitigate performance impacts by ensuring that only relevant changes are processed by each subscriber.

Security is another key aspect of LDAP change notifications. Connections used for receiving notifications should be secured with SSL/TLS to protect the confidentiality and integrity of directory data during transmission. Additionally, clients subscribing to change notifications should use dedicated service accounts with read-only permissions scoped to the specific directory subtrees they monitor. This principle of least privilege minimizes the attack surface and reduces the risk of accidental or malicious directory modifications by notification consumers.

LDAP change notifications can also integrate with messaging systems and event-driven architectures. For instance, notification consumers can forward change events to message brokers such as Apache Kafka, RabbitMQ, or AWS SNS, enabling other microservices or applications to process directory updates asynchronously. This approach supports decoupled architectures where different components of the IT environment can subscribe to specific LDAP event topics and react independently to changes. It also improves scalability by allowing multiple services to consume the same change events without creating redundant connections to the LDAP server.

Organizations that require robust change data capture and event processing often combine LDAP notifications with data transformation and enrichment workflows. A change event received from the LDAP server might trigger a series of automated tasks, such as validating the updated data against business rules, enriching it with information from external systems, and writing it to centralized data stores or audit logs. Automation platforms like Apache NiFi or custom Python-based pipelines can be used to orchestrate these workflows, increasing the value of change notifications beyond simple data synchronization.

LDAP change notifications are essential in modern IT ecosystems where real-time responsiveness and data consistency are paramount. They reduce reliance on inefficient polling mechanisms, decrease synchronization latency, and empower organizations to automate critical identity-related workflows across diverse applications and services. Whether used to streamline user provisioning, support security operations, or synchronize data across complex environments, LDAP change notifications form a key part of scalable and secure directory management strategies.

LDAP Password Policies

LDAP password policies are essential components of directory service management, providing administrators with the ability to enforce security requirements related to user authentication and password usage. In modern IT environments, where LDAP directories often serve as the central repository for user credentials across a wide range of applications and systems, implementing robust password policies is critical to reducing the risk of unauthorized access and strengthening the organization's overall security posture. LDAP password policies define the rules and constraints that govern how passwords are created, stored, validated, and expired within the directory.

At a high level, LDAP password policies address several key aspects of password management, including password complexity, minimum and maximum password lengths, password expiration, account lockout mechanisms, password history, and password change intervals. These rules ensure that users create strong passwords and change them regularly, while also providing controls to mitigate brute-force attacks and credential reuse.

Password complexity requirements are among the most common elements of LDAP password policies. Administrators can enforce rules requiring users to create passwords that include a combination of uppercase and lowercase letters, numbers, and special characters. By preventing the use of simple or easily guessable passwords, complexity requirements help protect against dictionary attacks and common credential stuffing techniques. Additionally, password length restrictions ensure that users create passwords with a minimum number of characters, making them more resistant to brute-force attempts.

Password expiration policies force users to change their passwords periodically, reducing the risk of long-term exposure if a password is compromised. Administrators can define the maximum password age, specifying how many days a password remains valid before the user is required to set a new one. Expired passwords typically trigger an LDAP control that prompts the user to change their password upon their next login. Some implementations also allow the configuration of minimum password age settings, which prevent users from immediately reusing old passwords after a forced change.

Password history is another critical control that prevents users from cycling through a small set of commonly used passwords. By retaining a history of previous passwords, LDAP servers can enforce policies that prohibit the reuse of recent passwords, encouraging users to create new and unique credentials during each password change cycle. The number of previous passwords stored in the history can be adjusted according to organizational security policies.

Account lockout mechanisms are designed to thwart brute-force attacks by temporarily disabling user accounts after a specified number of consecutive failed authentication attempts. LDAP servers can be configured to lock an account after a defined threshold, such as five or ten invalid password attempts, and to maintain the lock for a set duration or until manual administrative intervention. This policy limits the effectiveness of automated attacks that attempt to guess user credentials by cycling through large password dictionaries.

LDAP password policies often integrate with password quality modules that perform additional checks beyond basic complexity rules. These modules can include checks against lists of commonly used or breached passwords, preventing users from selecting credentials that are known to be insecure. Advanced implementations may also evaluate passwords for patterns, such as repeating characters or sequences like 123456, that weaken password strength. These checks help ensure that passwords meet not only length and character diversity requirements but also resist known attack techniques.

LDAP directories support password policies through various extensions and overlays. In OpenLDAP environments, the ppolicy overlay is commonly used to enforce password policies. The ppolicy overlay defines operational attributes within user entries that track password policy compliance, such as password expiration timestamps, account lockout status, and password failure counts. These attributes enable the LDAP server to apply password policies automatically during bind operations and password modifications.

Administrators can configure multiple password policies tailored to different user populations by leveraging policy subtrees or specific object classes. For example, service accounts or privileged users may be subject to more stringent password policies than standard users, requiring longer passwords, more frequent password changes, or shorter lockout thresholds. LDAP supports this granularity by applying policies based on user location within the directory hierarchy or by referencing specific policy entries through operational attributes.

Password policy enforcement can extend beyond the LDAP server itself to applications and systems that rely on the directory for authentication. When integrated properly, applications that perform LDAP binds can detect password policy violations and prompt users with appropriate actions, such as initiating a password reset process when a password has expired. This integration ensures a consistent user experience and centralizes password management within the LDAP directory, reducing fragmentation and administrative burden.

Security considerations are critical when implementing LDAP password policies. Passwords should always be stored using strong, salted hash algorithms such as SSHA, bcrypt, or Argon2, depending on the capabilities of the LDAP server. Plaintext password storage is never acceptable and represents a severe security risk. Password hashes must also be protected by robust access control lists, restricting access to sensitive attributes such as userPassword to only authorized administrative accounts or processes.

LDAP password policies should align with the organization's broader security framework and regulatory obligations. Standards such as NIST 800-63B, PCI DSS, and ISO/IEC 27001 often define minimum password length, complexity, and change frequency requirements that organizations must meet to remain compliant. Additionally, organizations must balance security with usability, ensuring that password policies are not overly restrictive or burdensome to users, which could lead to insecure workarounds such as writing passwords down or storing them in unsecured files.

Audit logging and monitoring play an essential role in password policy enforcement. LDAP servers should log password-related events, including successful and failed login attempts, password changes, and account lockouts. These logs provide valuable insights for security teams, supporting the detection of suspicious activity and the investigation of potential incidents. Integrating LDAP logs with centralized logging platforms or SIEM systems allows organizations to automate alerts for events such as repeated lockouts or anomalous password reset patterns.

Automated workflows can also enhance LDAP password policy compliance. For example, organizations can integrate LDAP with self-service password reset portals that enforce directory password policies while simplifying the user experience. These portals allow users to reset expired or forgotten passwords securely without requiring direct administrative intervention, reducing help desk workload and improving user satisfaction.

LDAP password policies are a cornerstone of secure and effective identity and access management. By defining and enforcing consistent rules for password creation, usage, and management, organizations can significantly reduce the risk of unauthorized access and improve the resilience of their directory infrastructure. Careful planning, thoughtful configuration, and ongoing monitoring are key to ensuring that password policies protect critical systems while supporting the operational needs of users and applications.

Customizing LDAP Schemas

Customizing LDAP schemas is a common and necessary task for organizations that need to extend the functionality of their directory services beyond the limitations of default schema definitions. An LDAP schema defines the structure of the directory data, including object classes, attributes, syntaxes, and matching rules. While most LDAP servers come with predefined standard schemas that support general identity and access management needs, organizations often require additional custom attributes or object classes to model their unique business processes, applications, and organizational structures. By customizing the LDAP schema, administrators can tailor the directory to meet specific operational requirements while maintaining data consistency and interoperability across systems.

The customization process begins with identifying the business or technical needs that cannot be addressed by existing schema elements. For example, an organization might need to store attributes such as employee badge numbers, application-specific roles, project codes, or custom metadata that do not exist in the standard schema. Before creating new schema elements, it is considered best practice to review and reuse existing object classes and attributes where possible. Extending the schema should be done cautiously and with a clear understanding of the impact on directory design, performance, and compatibility.

When creating custom object classes, administrators must decide whether to define structural, auxiliary, or abstract classes based on how the data will be used. A structural object class is the primary object class for an entry and defines its essential characteristics. An auxiliary object class supplements existing entries by adding additional attributes without changing the entry's core structure. For instance, if an organization already uses the inetOrgPerson structural object class for user accounts but needs to store additional attributes specific to a contractor population, it could create an auxiliary object class and apply it to relevant entries. This modular approach allows for flexibility and minimizes schema changes across unrelated entries.

Each custom object class and attribute requires a unique object identifier (OID). OIDs are hierarchical numeric values that ensure global uniqueness across schema definitions. Organizations should obtain a private OID arc from a registration authority or use a reserved arc for internal use. Consistently generating OIDs for custom schema elements helps prevent conflicts when integrating with external directories or applications. In addition to OIDs, administrators should assign meaningful names to object classes and attributes, adhering to naming conventions that reflect the organization's domain or project, such as acmeProjectCode or acmeContractorID.

Custom attributes require careful definition of their syntax and matching rules. Syntax specifies the data type and format of the attribute values, such as directoryString, integer, or generalizedTime. Matching rules define how LDAP servers compare attribute values during search operations. For instance, caseIgnoreMatch might be applied to string attributes to perform case-insensitive comparisons, while integerMatch ensures exact numerical matching for integer attributes. Choosing the correct syntax and matching rules improves search accuracy, enhances query performance, and ensures the directory behaves as expected under various use cases.

Once custom object classes and attributes are defined, they are added to the LDAP schema through schema configuration files or dynamic updates, depending on the directory implementation. In OpenLDAP, for example, schemas are often written in LDIF format, where each object class and attribute is defined using a structured set of directives. The schema file is then loaded into the directory using slapadd or integrated directly into the cn=schema subtree via LDAP modify operations. Changes to the schema must be validated to ensure compliance with LDAP standards and to prevent directory server startup failures caused by malformed schema entries.

Customizing the schema also involves updating documentation and processes related to directory management. Administrators should maintain clear and detailed records of custom schema elements, including their OIDs, descriptions, attribute types, usage guidelines, and associated object classes. This documentation ensures that all stakeholders, including developers, security teams, and system integrators, understand the purpose and implementation details of each custom element. Well-documented schemas also facilitate troubleshooting, schema auditing, and future enhancements to the directory.

Schema customization must consider the impact on interoperability. Applications and systems that interact with the LDAP directory may rely on standard schemas and may not recognize custom attributes without additional configuration. For example, a web application using LDAP for user authentication may require modifications to its LDAP queries to retrieve newly added custom attributes or to adjust input validation rules. Similarly, synchronization tools and identity federation platforms may need to be updated to map custom attributes correctly between the LDAP directory and external identity providers, such as Azure AD or Okta.

Performance optimization is a key consideration when extending LDAP schemas. Custom attributes that are frequently used in search filters should be indexed appropriately to reduce search latency and minimize directory server load. Over-indexing, however, can lead to excessive disk I/O and increased memory consumption, so administrators must carefully balance indexing needs with resource availability. Custom attributes that are intended solely for informational purposes and are not part of search queries may not require indexing at all.

Security is another critical aspect of schema customization. Access control policies must be updated to ensure that custom attributes are protected according to their sensitivity. For example, if a custom attribute stores personally identifiable information or internal classification codes, administrators should apply strict ACLs to restrict access to authorized personnel only. Additionally, write permissions should be limited to trusted service accounts or administrators, reducing the risk of accidental or malicious modifications.

In replicated environments, custom schema updates must be propagated consistently across all LDAP servers. Inconsistencies in schema definitions can cause replication errors or data conflicts.

Administrators should implement change management procedures to deploy schema updates in a controlled and coordinated manner, ensuring that all directory nodes are updated simultaneously and that the integrity of the replication topology is preserved.

Testing is a fundamental step in the schema customization process. Before deploying custom schema elements to production environments, administrators should validate them in a staging environment that mirrors production as closely as possible. This testing phase should include creating sample directory entries that use the custom object classes and attributes, performing search and modification operations, and verifying that applications interacting with the directory function correctly with the new schema in place.

Customizing LDAP schemas provides organizations with the flexibility to model their directory data according to specific operational requirements while extending the utility of the directory service beyond basic user and group management. When approached with careful planning and attention to best practices, schema customization enhances the directory's ability to support business processes, improve data management workflows, and integrate seamlessly with both internal applications and external systems. A well-designed and thoroughly documented schema not only addresses current requirements but also provides a scalable foundation for future growth and evolving identity management needs.

Using LDAP in Enterprise Environments

Using LDAP in enterprise environments is a fundamental practice that enables organizations to centralize identity management, simplify authentication processes, and secure access to a wide array of systems and applications. As enterprises scale, the complexity of managing users, groups, and policies across diverse platforms increases exponentially. LDAP provides a unified directory service that serves as the backbone for user authentication, authorization, and directory lookups, facilitating efficient and secure identity and access management (IAM) across an organization's infrastructure.

One of the core benefits of LDAP in enterprise environments is its ability to consolidate identity data into a single authoritative directory. In large organizations, employees, contractors, partners, and service accounts often need access to multiple applications, networks, and resources. Without a centralized directory service, user accounts may be duplicated across disparate systems, leading to inconsistencies, security vulnerabilities, and administrative overhead. LDAP provides a central repository where all user identities, group memberships, organizational hierarchies, and access control attributes are stored and maintained, creating a single source of truth for identity data.

In an enterprise context, LDAP is typically integrated with a wide range of business-critical systems, including email servers, file servers, ERP platforms, customer relationship management (CRM) systems, and intranet portals. By configuring these systems to authenticate users against the LDAP directory, organizations can implement single sign-on (SSO) capabilities, reducing password fatigue and enhancing security. Users can log in to multiple systems using the same set of credentials, while administrators manage all accounts from a centralized LDAP infrastructure.

LDAP's flexibility allows it to support various directory structures and naming conventions tailored to the organization's needs. Enterprises often design their LDAP directory to reflect their organizational chart, using a hierarchical model that segments users into organizational units (OUs) based on departments, regions, or business units. This structure facilitates delegation of administrative responsibilities, as different teams or regional offices can be assigned control over specific OUs without impacting the broader directory. The hierarchical nature of LDAP also supports efficient search operations, as queries can be scoped to specific subtrees of the directory.

Security is a key priority in enterprise environments, and LDAP plays a critical role in enforcing access control policies. LDAP directories enable granular control over who can access specific resources based on group memberships, roles, or attribute values. Enterprises commonly use LDAP groups to define permissions for applications, systems, and services. For example, members of an LDAP group such as cn=finance,ou=groups,dc=example,dc=com may be granted access to financial systems and data, while members of cn=developers may have elevated privileges within development environments. These group-based permissions are centrally managed and propagated to integrated systems, simplifying administration and reducing the likelihood of privilege creep.

LDAP directories also integrate seamlessly with network security mechanisms. Many organizations configure VPNs, wireless networks, and remote access gateways to authenticate users against LDAP, ensuring that only authorized users can access internal networks. Additionally, LDAP is often combined with multi-factor authentication (MFA) solutions, requiring users to provide a second authentication factor, such as a time-based one-time password (TOTP) or hardware token, in addition to their LDAP credentials. This layered approach strengthens enterprise security and helps meet compliance requirements imposed by regulations such as PCI DSS, HIPAA, and ISO 27001.

Replication is another critical feature of LDAP deployments in enterprise environments. To ensure high availability and performance across geographically distributed locations, organizations deploy LDAP replicas or implement multi-master replication. This design allows users in remote offices or branches to authenticate against local LDAP servers, reducing latency and dependency on a single data center. In the event of a server failure or network outage, LDAP replication ensures that authentication services remain operational, supporting business continuity and disaster recovery objectives.

Enterprises also rely on LDAP to automate identity lifecycle management processes. As employees join, move within, or leave an organization, their LDAP accounts and associated permissions must be provisioned, modified, or deprovisioned accordingly. Identity management solutions or custom automation scripts integrate with LDAP to enforce these changes consistently across all connected systems. For example, onboarding workflows automatically create new LDAP accounts, assign appropriate group memberships based on job roles, and trigger provisioning processes for cloud applications and internal systems. Conversely, when an employee departs, their LDAP account can be immediately disabled, and associated entitlements revoked to prevent unauthorized access.

LDAP's extensibility is valuable for enterprises that require custom attributes or object classes to support business-specific processes. Administrators can extend the LDAP schema to include additional data fields relevant to the organization, such as employee ID numbers, contractor classifications, cost center codes, or application-specific roles. These custom attributes enrich directory entries and provide greater flexibility when building access control policies, generating reports, or integrating with third-party systems.

Monitoring and logging are essential for enterprise LDAP deployments. LDAP servers generate logs that capture authentication attempts, bind operations, search queries, and modifications to directory data. These logs provide visibility into directory activity, supporting security auditing, compliance reporting, and incident response efforts. Integrating LDAP logs with Security Information and Event Management (SIEM) platforms enhances threat detection capabilities, allowing security teams to identify and respond to anomalies such as brute-force attacks, unauthorized access attempts, or privilege escalations.

Performance optimization is a constant focus in enterprise environments where LDAP servers must handle thousands of concurrent users and high query volumes. Administrators fine-tune LDAP configurations by indexing frequently queried attributes, adjusting cache settings, and balancing workloads across multiple servers. Load balancers or global traffic managers are often deployed to distribute LDAP queries across servers located in different regions, improving responsiveness and fault tolerance.

In modern enterprise environments, LDAP is increasingly integrated with cloud platforms and identity-as-a-service (IDaaS) providers. Hybrid identity models synchronize LDAP directories with cloud-based directories such as Azure Active Directory, enabling organizations to manage on-premises and cloud identities from a unified platform. LDAP also supports federation with single sign-on solutions that bridge the gap between traditional directory services and SaaS applications. By combining LDAP with modern authentication protocols like SAML or OpenID Connect, enterprises can extend centralized identity management to the cloud while maintaining compatibility with legacy systems.

Using LDAP in enterprise environments is indispensable for achieving centralized, secure, and scalable identity and access management. Its ability to serve as the backbone of authentication and directory services enables organizations to streamline operations, reduce risk, and support business agility across complex IT landscapes. Whether managing thousands of employee accounts, securing mission-critical applications, or integrating with modern cloud platforms, LDAP remains a cornerstone of enterprise IAM strategies.

Migrating from Legacy Directory Systems

Migrating from legacy directory systems to a modern LDAP-based infrastructure is a complex but necessary process for organizations seeking to improve security, scalability, and interoperability in their identity and access management (IAM) environments. Legacy directory systems, such as proprietary or outdated directory services, often lack the flexibility, performance, and integration capabilities required by contemporary IT landscapes. As enterprises modernize their infrastructure, the need to transition from these legacy systems to standards-based LDAP directories becomes a critical project that demands careful planning, risk mitigation, and strategic execution.

The migration process typically begins with a comprehensive assessment of the existing directory environment. This assessment includes identifying all legacy directory systems in use, documenting their data models, analyzing directory structures, and inventorying all integrated applications and services. Understanding the dependencies between these systems and the directory is essential to ensure a smooth transition. Many legacy directories have unique schemas or custom attributes that may not map directly to standard LDAP schemas, requiring organizations to develop a migration strategy that includes schema normalization or customization.

Once the assessment is complete, organizations must select the target LDAP directory platform. Common choices include OpenLDAP, Microsoft Active Directory, or other LDAP-compliant directory servers, depending on organizational requirements, existing infrastructure, and the desired integration with other enterprise systems. The selection process should consider factors such as scalability, replication capabilities, support for access control policies, high availability options, and compatibility with applications that will consume directory services.

Data migration is the core phase of the project and involves transferring directory entries, object classes, and attributes from the legacy system to the new LDAP environment. This step often requires transforming data to conform to the target LDAP schema. For instance, a legacy directory may use proprietary attribute names or unconventional object classes that need to be remapped to standard LDAP attributes such as uid, cn, or mail. Data transformation can be achieved through custom scripts or migration tools that extract, transform, and load (ETL) directory entries into the new system while preserving data integrity and consistency.

During migration, organizations must address password handling and authentication considerations. Legacy directories may store passwords using different hashing algorithms or encryption mechanisms that are incompatible with the new LDAP server. In such cases, it may be necessary to prompt users to reset their passwords upon first login to the new system or to migrate password hashes using compatible algorithms where possible. Security is paramount during this step, as improper handling of password data can expose sensitive credentials to risk.

Testing plays a critical role in migration success. Organizations should create a staging environment that mirrors the production infrastructure, allowing administrators to validate data migration scripts, verify schema mappings, and perform thorough functional testing of LDAP integrations with applications and systems. Test scenarios should include authenticating users against the new LDAP directory, validating group memberships and access control policies, and ensuring that applications can successfully retrieve directory attributes as required. This testing phase also helps uncover potential performance bottlenecks and interoperability issues before they impact production environments.

A phased migration approach is often recommended to minimize disruption to business operations. In a phased strategy, directory data is migrated incrementally, starting with non-critical systems or specific organizational units. This allows administrators to gain experience with the migration process, address unforeseen challenges, and adjust the strategy before migrating critical systems or the entire user population. Phased migrations also provide the flexibility to run the legacy and new directories in parallel during the transition period, reducing the risk of service outages and enabling gradual application cutovers.

Replication and synchronization tools can assist with maintaining data consistency between the legacy and new LDAP directories during the migration window. Some organizations implement temporary synchronization mechanisms to propagate updates from the legacy system to the new directory, ensuring that changes made to user accounts or group memberships in the legacy environment are reflected in the target LDAP server until the migration is fully completed. This bidirectional or unidirectional synchronization minimizes data drift and facilitates smoother cutovers for integrated applications.

Communication with stakeholders is essential throughout the migration project. Users must be informed about any changes to login procedures, password reset requirements, or access to applications that rely on the directory service. IT teams should coordinate closely with business units to schedule migration activities during low-usage periods and to provide support resources for users encountering issues after the transition. Well-documented migration guides, FAQs, and help desk procedures can significantly reduce confusion and improve user adoption.

Post-migration tasks focus on decommissioning the legacy directory system and optimizing the new LDAP environment. Once all users and applications have been successfully migrated and are operating normally, administrators can begin retiring the old directory servers, ensuring that all sensitive data is securely erased according to organizational policies and regulatory requirements. At this stage, LDAP directory configurations should be reviewed and fine-tuned to enhance performance, enforce access control policies, and enable auditing and monitoring features.

Security hardening of the new LDAP environment is also a top priority. Administrators should implement SSL/TLS encryption for all LDAP communications, enforce strong password policies, and apply role-based access controls to restrict directory modifications to authorized accounts only. Integrating LDAP logs with centralized monitoring tools and SIEM platforms ensures that identity-related events are continuously monitored for signs of suspicious activity.

Migrating from legacy directory systems to LDAP can deliver substantial benefits, including improved interoperability with modern applications, support for industry-standard protocols, and enhanced scalability to meet growing business demands. The new LDAP environment can also integrate seamlessly with cloud identity platforms, federated authentication systems, and single sign-on solutions, enabling organizations to adopt hybrid and multi-cloud architectures without sacrificing centralized identity management.

Successful migration projects require careful planning, technical expertise, and coordination across IT, security, and business teams. By taking a methodical approach that prioritizes data integrity, user experience, and security, organizations can transition from legacy directory systems to a modern LDAP infrastructure that serves as a foundation for secure and efficient identity management in today's dynamic enterprise environments.

Case Study: LDAP in a Large Organization

In a multinational corporation with tens of thousands of employees operating in multiple regions, the need for a scalable, secure, and highly available identity management solution is paramount. This organization, with offices spread across North America, Europe, and Asia, faced challenges with fragmented identity systems, inconsistent access control policies, and administrative overhead caused by managing multiple independent directories. After evaluating various options, the company decided to implement a centralized LDAP directory to unify its global identity and access management processes. The deployment of LDAP became a transformative project that enabled streamlined operations, improved security, and greater agility across the enterprise.

Prior to LDAP implementation, the company maintained several disparate legacy directory systems in different regions, each supporting localized applications and user populations. These siloed directories made it difficult to enforce consistent security policies or provide seamless authentication to global applications. Users often needed multiple accounts to access systems across different regions, leading to password fatigue, increased help desk requests, and difficulties maintaining audit trails. The lack of a centralized identity source also hindered the organization's ability to integrate with cloud services and modern applications, which required standardized authentication mechanisms.

The project began with a comprehensive assessment of the existing directories, application dependencies, and user populations. The company chose OpenLDAP as the backbone of its global directory service, attracted by its flexibility, open-source nature, and support for customization. To design a directory structure that aligned with the organization's business model, the team created a hierarchical Directory Information Tree (DIT) that mirrored the corporate organizational structure. Organizational units (OUs) were established to represent each geographic region, business division, and functional department, enabling delegation of administrative rights and facilitating localized directory management while preserving a unified global structure.

Schema customization was a critical part of the implementation. The organization needed to support attributes unique to its operations, such as project codes, cost center identifiers, and employee types distinguishing full-time employees, contractors, and partners. A set of auxiliary object classes was created to extend standard schemas like inetOrgPerson, allowing the storage of custom attributes without affecting application compatibility. The directory design also introduced specialized object classes for service accounts and application integrations, ensuring that non-human identities were managed separately from user accounts with clearly defined access policies.

Replication and high availability were crucial requirements for this global deployment. The organization implemented a multi-master replication model, deploying LDAP servers in major data centers located in New York, London, Frankfurt, Singapore, and Tokyo. This design ensured local availability and fast response times for users in each region, while multi-master replication kept directory data synchronized across all locations. Load balancers were configured in each data center to distribute client requests across available LDAP servers, enhancing fault tolerance and load distribution.

To secure directory traffic, all LDAP communications were encrypted using TLS, and strict access control lists were configured to limit read and write operations based on user roles and administrative responsibilities. Service accounts used for application integrations were granted access only to the specific attributes and subtrees required for their operation, following the principle of least privilege. Additionally, an extensive logging and monitoring framework was implemented, forwarding LDAP logs to a centralized SIEM platform for continuous security monitoring, anomaly detection, and compliance reporting.

Integrating LDAP with existing enterprise applications was a multi-phase process. Business-critical systems, including the company's ERP, CRM, and internal collaboration tools, were configured to authenticate users directly against the centralized LDAP directory. The IT team developed custom connectors and scripts to map application-specific roles and permissions to LDAP groups, simplifying user provisioning workflows. Additionally, VPN gateways, wireless networks, and remote access platforms were integrated with LDAP to provide secure authentication for remote and mobile users.

A key benefit realized after the deployment was the streamlined onboarding and offboarding process. With a centralized directory in place, new employee accounts were automatically created in LDAP based on HR system triggers, and group memberships were assigned according to job role, department, and location. When employees left the organization, their LDAP accounts were promptly disabled, and their access to applications and systems was revoked automatically, reducing the risk of orphaned accounts and unauthorized access.

The LDAP infrastructure also enabled the company to extend its identity management capabilities to cloud platforms. By synchronizing LDAP with Azure Active Directory and integrating with a federated SSO solution, the organization was able to provide secure, seamless access to SaaS applications such as Office 365, Salesforce, and ServiceNow. Users benefited from single sign-on functionality across both on-premises and cloud-based systems, reducing password fatigue and improving productivity.

Performance improvements were noticeable across the enterprise. Centralized directory services eliminated the delays and inconsistencies caused by fragmented identity systems. Directory searches, user authentications, and group membership lookups became faster and more reliable, particularly for globally distributed teams accessing applications hosted in different regions. The LDAP implementation also reduced help desk workload, as password resets and user provisioning tasks were streamlined and largely automated through integration with existing ITSM tools and self-service portals.

From a governance and compliance perspective, the centralized LDAP directory enabled the company to enforce standardized password policies, access control rules, and audit procedures across all regions and business units. Regular audits of group memberships, service accounts, and directory changes were conducted using LDAP reports, improving the organization's ability to meet regulatory requirements such as GDPR, SOX, and ISO 27001.

As the LDAP deployment matured, the company expanded its usage to support additional initiatives, including microservices architectures and DevOps workflows. Kubernetes clusters were integrated with LDAP for user authentication, and CI/CD pipelines leveraged LDAP to manage service accounts and enforce access policies. LDAP also served as the identity source for internal APIs, ensuring that services followed consistent access controls regardless of their deployment environment.

The successful deployment of LDAP in this large organization highlights how centralized directory services can transform identity and access management at scale. By addressing the challenges of fragmented identity systems, inconsistent policies, and administrative complexity, LDAP became a foundational element of the company's modern IT strategy. The implementation not only improved operational efficiency and security but also provided the agility needed to support the evolving demands of a dynamic global business.

LDAP Compliance and Regulatory Considerations

LDAP compliance and regulatory considerations are essential factors for organizations operating in sectors subject to legal, industry, or contractual obligations regarding data privacy, security, and access management. As LDAP directories often serve as centralized repositories for sensitive identity information, including usernames, passwords, roles, and personal attributes, they must be designed, configured, and maintained in alignment with various compliance frameworks to mitigate risk and ensure legal adherence. Failure to properly secure and manage LDAP environments can lead to significant regulatory penalties, reputational damage, and operational disruptions.

One of the most important regulatory considerations for LDAP directories involves data protection and privacy laws. Regulations such as the General Data Protection Regulation (GDPR) in the European Union, the California Consumer Privacy Act (CCPA) in the United States, and Brazil's Lei Geral de Proteção de Dados (LGPD) require organizations to implement appropriate technical and organizational measures to protect personal data. Since LDAP directories often store personally identifiable information (PII) such as employee names, email addresses, phone numbers, and job titles, organizations must ensure that directory data is processed and stored in a secure and compliant manner.

Access control is one of the foundational elements of LDAP compliance. Regulatory frameworks frequently mandate that organizations limit access to personal data based on the principle of least privilege. LDAP administrators must configure detailed access control lists (ACLs) that restrict read, write, and modify operations to authorized personnel and applications only. For example, general users may only be allowed to view their own directory attributes, while HR personnel or IT administrators may have broader permissions over organizational units containing user data. Sensitive attributes, such as userPassword, socialSecurityNumber, or other regulatory-protected information, should be protected by stricter ACLs to reduce the risk of unauthorized access.

Secure transmission of LDAP data is another critical consideration. Regulatory standards typically require organizations to safeguard personal data during transmission over networks. LDAP implementations must enforce SSL/TLS encryption for all communications between clients and servers, as well as between replicated servers in distributed environments. This protects sensitive information from interception, eavesdropping, or tampering by unauthorized parties. LDAP configurations should disable insecure protocols such as plain-text LDAP (port 389 without StartTLS) in favor of secure alternatives like LDAPS (port 636) or LDAP over StartTLS.

Password policies enforced within the LDAP directory must also comply with regulatory and industry standards. Frameworks such as NIST SP 800-63B, PCI DSS, and ISO/IEC 27001 define requirements for password complexity, expiration, and reuse prevention. LDAP password policies should mandate strong, unique passwords for all accounts, enforce minimum and maximum password ages, and prevent the reuse of recent passwords. For service accounts or privileged user accounts, organizations may also implement additional measures such as requiring multi-factor authentication (MFA) alongside LDAP credentials.

Logging and auditing are vital to ensuring LDAP compliance with various regulatory mandates. Organizations must maintain comprehensive logs of all directory access events, including successful and failed login attempts, user account modifications, group membership changes, and ACL updates. These logs provide critical evidence for forensic investigations, internal audits, and compliance reporting. To support compliance efforts, LDAP logs should be integrated into centralized security information and event management (SIEM) systems where they can be correlated with other infrastructure logs, monitored for anomalies, and retained according to applicable data retention policies.

Data minimization is a further requirement outlined in regulations such as GDPR, which stipulates that organizations collect and store only the data necessary for specific processing purposes. LDAP directory entries should be reviewed to ensure that they do not store excessive or irrelevant attributes. For example, a directory used solely for authentication purposes may not require attributes related to HR records or physical addresses. Minimizing the amount of personal data stored in LDAP not only aids compliance but also reduces the potential impact of a data breach.

Data retention and deletion policies also play a role in regulatory compliance. Personal data stored within LDAP directories should not be retained indefinitely unless justified by business or legal requirements. Organizations must implement processes to periodically review and remove obsolete or unnecessary directory entries, such as accounts belonging to former employees or expired service accounts. Automated deprovisioning workflows, triggered by HR systems or identity governance platforms, can ensure that LDAP accounts are promptly deactivated and purged when no longer needed, helping meet data retention obligations.

Cross-border data transfers are an additional concern in global organizations. If LDAP directories replicate or share data between servers located in different countries, regulatory requirements for international data transfers must be considered. For example, GDPR imposes restrictions on transferring personal data outside of the European Economic Area (EEA) to jurisdictions that lack adequate data protection laws. Organizations may need to implement mechanisms such as standard contractual clauses, binding corporate rules, or ensure reliance on adequacy decisions when replicating LDAP data across international boundaries.

Incident response and breach notification obligations are closely tied to LDAP security. In the event of unauthorized access to LDAP directories or a data breach affecting personal information stored within them, organizations may be legally required to notify affected individuals, regulatory authorities, or business partners within specific timeframes. Having an LDAP-specific incident response plan that includes rapid log review, access revocation procedures, and predefined notification templates can streamline compliance with breach notification requirements.

Compliance frameworks may also require periodic risk assessments and penetration testing of LDAP environments. These assessments help identify vulnerabilities such as weak password policies, unpatched software, or misconfigured access controls. LDAP servers should be subject to regular vulnerability scans, configuration audits, and security hardening measures, ensuring they remain resilient against evolving threats.

Vendor and third-party integrations with LDAP also raise compliance considerations. Organizations must ensure that any external applications, SaaS platforms, or service providers accessing LDAP data comply with contractual and regulatory obligations regarding data protection. This may involve conducting due diligence, reviewing third-party security certifications, or implementing data processing agreements that define roles, responsibilities, and security expectations.

Compliance is not limited to technical controls but also encompasses policy development and staff training. Administrators managing LDAP environments should receive regular training on security best practices, regulatory requirements, and internal policies related to directory data handling. Organizations should maintain clear documentation outlining acceptable use, access management processes, and incident response procedures for LDAP systems.

LDAP compliance and regulatory considerations require a multi-faceted approach that combines technical safeguards, administrative controls, and continuous monitoring. By aligning LDAP directory practices with relevant regulations and standards, organizations can protect sensitive identity data, meet legal obligations, and reduce exposure to security risks. As regulatory landscapes evolve, maintaining LDAP compliance is an ongoing responsibility that requires vigilance, proactive management, and collaboration between IT, security, and compliance teams.

The Future of LDAP

The future of LDAP is shaped by the continuous evolution of enterprise IT environments, the growing emphasis on hybrid and multi-cloud architectures, and the increasing complexity of identity and access management. Despite being a protocol that has existed for decades, LDAP continues to play a critical role as the backbone for directory services across a wide variety of industries and sectors. As organizations move towards distributed, cloud-native, and zero-trust security models, LDAP is adapting to remain relevant by integrating with modern technologies, protocols, and architectures.

One of the most significant trends influencing the future of LDAP is the continued shift toward cloud computing and hybrid IT infrastructures. Enterprises are migrating applications and services to public cloud platforms while maintaining on-premises systems for legacy workloads and regulatory compliance requirements. In this hybrid landscape, LDAP directories are evolving to serve as central hubs that synchronize identity data across on-premises and cloud environments. Cloud-native directory services that offer LDAP interfaces, such as AWS Directory Service or Azure Active Directory Domain Services, are becoming common solutions that extend traditional LDAP capabilities into cloud platforms. This trend allows organizations to leverage LDAP's familiar data models and protocols while benefiting from the scalability, high availability, and managed services provided by cloud vendors.

Another critical factor shaping LDAP's trajectory is the growing demand for interoperability with modern identity protocols. While LDAP excels in providing centralized directory services, modern applications increasingly rely on protocols such as OAuth2, OpenID Connect, and SAML for federated identity management and single sign-on capabilities. To stay relevant, LDAP is increasingly being integrated with identity federation platforms and access management solutions that bridge the gap between LDAP and these newer protocols. This integration enables organizations to continue using LDAP as the authoritative identity source while supporting seamless authentication and authorization workflows across SaaS platforms, APIs, and cloud-native applications.

LDAP's role in zero-trust architectures is another area where its relevance is expanding. Zero-trust models assume that no user or system is inherently trustworthy, and access must be continuously verified based on identity, device health, and context. LDAP directories serve as a foundational element of zero-trust environments by providing reliable and authoritative identity data that informs policy engines, identity providers, and access brokers. LDAP attributes such as group memberships, user roles, and organizational hierarchies feed into dynamic access control decisions, enabling granular, policy-driven access management aligned with zero-trust principles.

The integration of LDAP with automation, DevOps, and Infrastructure as Code (IaC) practices is also influencing its future direction. Organizations are increasingly automating the provisioning, management, and deprovisioning of LDAP accounts, group memberships, and access policies using automation tools like Ansible, Terraform, and CI/CD pipelines. By treating LDAP configuration and directory data as code, administrators can enforce consistency, accelerate deployments, and reduce the risk of human error. This trend is further reinforced by the rise of containers and microservices architectures, where LDAP is used to manage service accounts, application identities, and secure communication between distributed components.

Security enhancements and evolving compliance requirements are prompting ongoing developments in LDAP implementations. The increasing sophistication of cyber threats has led to greater emphasis on secure communication channels, encryption standards, and auditing capabilities within directory services. LDAP servers are adapting by supporting modern TLS configurations, strong hashing algorithms for password storage, and tighter access controls that align with industry standards and regulatory mandates such as GDPR, HIPAA, and PCI DSS. Additionally, organizations are integrating LDAP logs with advanced monitoring and security information and event management (SIEM) platforms to achieve real-time visibility and threat detection within directory environments.

The rise of machine learning and artificial intelligence in IT operations and cybersecurity may also impact LDAP's future. As organizations adopt AI-driven identity analytics platforms, LDAP directories will increasingly provide the raw identity and access data needed to fuel behavioral analysis and anomaly detection. AI engines can leverage LDAP data to identify unusual access patterns, detect insider threats, or automate identity governance processes, elevating LDAP's role beyond traditional directory services into proactive security and compliance enforcement.

LDAP is also evolving to support new use cases and deployment models. Lightweight LDAP servers designed for edge computing environments are gaining traction, allowing directory services to be deployed in distributed, resource-constrained environments such as remote branches, industrial IoT networks, and mobile edge clouds. These lightweight implementations maintain LDAP's hierarchical and flexible data model while providing the performance and footprint required for edge deployments, helping organizations extend identity services closer to where applications and users reside.

The open-source community plays a pivotal role in shaping the future of LDAP. Projects such as OpenLDAP continue to receive updates, feature enhancements, and security patches from a global community of contributors. Innovations such as dynamic configuration backends, modernized schema management tools, and enhanced replication mechanisms ensure that LDAP remains a robust and adaptable technology for contemporary IT needs. In addition, commercial vendors are introducing LDAP-compatible products with added features such as RESTful APIs, graphical administration consoles, and seamless integration with identity governance and administration (IGA) platforms.

LDAP's future is also being influenced by its role in digital transformation initiatives. As organizations modernize their identity and access management frameworks, LDAP directories serve as the foundational data layer that supports user-centric digital services, customer identity and access management (CIAM) platforms, and cross-enterprise collaborations. The demand for secure, scalable, and interoperable identity services will ensure LDAP's continued relevance as organizations expand their digital footprints and adopt cloud-native, multi-cloud, and hybrid operating models.

Looking ahead, LDAP will continue to coexist with emerging identity technologies and protocols rather than being replaced outright. Its strengths as a highly structured, hierarchical directory service make it an indispensable component of many enterprise IT ecosystems. By adapting to new integration models, security expectations, and automation frameworks, LDAP will remain a key enabler of secure and efficient identity management across both legacy systems and modern digital platforms. As enterprises balance tradition with innovation, LDAP's flexibility and proven reliability will ensure its role as a vital tool in the evolving identity landscape.

Emerging Trends in Directory Services

Emerging trends in directory services are being driven by rapid technological advancements, evolving security threats, and the continuous shift toward cloud-native and hybrid infrastructures. As organizations modernize their IT ecosystems, directory services are undergoing a transformation to meet new demands for scalability, flexibility, and integration with diverse applications and platforms. The traditional role of directory services as centralized repositories for user accounts and organizational structures is expanding, as they now play a pivotal part in complex identity and access management (IAM) strategies, zero-trust security models, and digital transformation initiatives.

One of the most notable trends in directory services is the growing convergence of directories with cloud-based identity providers and identity-as-a-service (IDaaS) platforms. As enterprises increasingly adopt public cloud services and SaaS applications, there is a demand for directory solutions that seamlessly bridge on-premises LDAP directories with cloud-native identity systems. Organizations are using synchronization tools to link traditional directories, such as Active Directory or OpenLDAP, with cloud directories like Azure Active Directory, Google Cloud Identity, or AWS Directory Service. This hybrid approach allows organizations to maintain centralized identity management across both legacy applications and modern cloud services, supporting single sign-on (SSO), identity federation, and policy enforcement across environments.

Another emerging trend is the integration of directory services into zero-trust security architectures. Zero-trust models require continuous verification of users, devices, and workloads based on identity and contextual data. Directory services, therefore, are no longer static repositories but dynamic participants in access control decisions. Modern directories provide attributes and group memberships that feed into zero-trust policy engines and microsegmentation strategies. These policies dictate granular access rules based on user roles, device health, location, and behavior. Directory services are becoming integral to real-time identity verification and the enforcement of least privilege principles at the application, network, and infrastructure levels.

Decentralized identity is another trend gaining momentum and influencing directory services. The rise of self-sovereign identity (SSI) and blockchain-based identity frameworks introduces new ways to manage and validate identities without relying on a single, centralized directory. In decentralized identity models, users control their credentials and selectively share them with service providers through verifiable credentials. While decentralized identity solutions are still maturing, they present a paradigm shift from traditional directory services by emphasizing user privacy, portability, and cryptographic assurance. Directory services are expected to integrate with these decentralized ecosystems, supporting hybrid identity models that balance central control with user autonomy.

Directory services are also being reshaped by the increasing adoption of APIs and directory-as-a-service (DaaS) solutions. Traditional LDAP protocols, while robust and widely adopted, are being supplemented with RESTful APIs and GraphQL interfaces to simplify integration with modern web and mobile applications. This trend aligns with the broader shift toward API-driven architectures, where developers require lightweight, easy-to-consume interfaces to directory data. DaaS providers are offering fully managed directory solutions that expose REST APIs, enabling organizations to offload directory infrastructure management while maintaining access to scalable, cloud-based directories for authentication, authorization, and user data storage.

The role of directory services in supporting DevOps and automation workflows is another trend shaping the landscape. As organizations adopt Infrastructure as Code (IaC) practices and continuous delivery pipelines, directory management is becoming increasingly automated. Tools such as Ansible, Terraform, and Kubernetes Operators are being used to provision and configure directory entries, service accounts, and access controls as part of automated deployment pipelines. By codifying directory configurations, enterprises ensure consistency across environments, reduce the risk of configuration drift, and accelerate application delivery while embedding security and compliance controls into the DevOps lifecycle.

Identity governance and compliance requirements are also driving the evolution of directory services. Regulations such as GDPR, CCPA, HIPAA, and SOX impose strict requirements for data protection, access control, and auditability. Directory services are integrating more closely with identity governance and administration (IGA) platforms to automate processes such as user provisioning, entitlement reviews, and policy enforcement. Modern directories now include enhanced auditing, reporting, and workflow capabilities to facilitate regulatory compliance and streamline identity lifecycle management across hybrid IT environments.

Another emerging trend is the focus on identity analytics and machine learning in directory environments. Organizations are leveraging AI and machine learning tools to analyze directory data, user behavior patterns, and access requests to detect anomalies and identify potential security risks. Identity analytics platforms can integrate with directory services to flag unusual login times, privilege escalations, or deviations from standard access patterns, enabling proactive incident response and risk mitigation. As cyber threats grow more sophisticated, directory services will continue to serve as critical data sources for AI-driven security and governance tools.

The integration of directory services with Internet of Things (IoT) ecosystems is another area of growth. As organizations deploy IoT devices across industries such as manufacturing, healthcare, and transportation, directory services are being extended to manage device identities alongside human users. Directories provide a centralized repository for storing device attributes, access credentials, and trust relationships, supporting secure onboarding and communication between IoT devices and backend systems. This trend is leading to the evolution of directories into identity platforms that handle heterogeneous identities, including users, devices, services, and applications.

Directory services are also being influenced by the growing importance of mobile and remote workforces. The rise of bring-your-own-device (BYOD) policies and global distributed teams requires directory services to support secure, seamless access to corporate resources from any location. Directories are being integrated with identity-aware proxies, secure access service edge (SASE) platforms, and endpoint detection and response (EDR) solutions to extend identity-based access controls to remote users. This ensures that directory-driven authentication and authorization mechanisms remain effective, regardless of where users connect from or which devices they use.

Finally, the focus on scalability and performance continues to shape directory service development. As organizations onboard more users, devices, and applications, directory services must scale horizontally to handle increased query volumes and authentication requests without compromising performance. Modern directory servers are incorporating distributed architectures, multi-master replication, and sharding techniques to improve resilience, reduce latency, and ensure high availability across global deployments.

The directory services landscape is rapidly evolving to meet the demands of modern IT environments. From hybrid identity models and zero-trust integrations to decentralized identity and API-driven access, directory services are expanding far beyond their traditional roles. As organizations continue to adopt cloud, automation, and AI-driven technologies, directory services will remain a foundational component of secure, scalable, and intelligent identity management strategies that enable innovation while safeguarding sensitive data and critical systems.

Common Pitfalls in LDAP Deployments

Deploying LDAP in enterprise environments is a task that requires careful planning, configuration, and ongoing maintenance. Despite the protocol's flexibility and maturity, organizations often encounter a variety of challenges that can impact security, performance, and the overall success of the deployment. Understanding the most common pitfalls in LDAP deployments is essential for avoiding costly mistakes and ensuring that directory services remain a reliable and secure foundation for identity and access management.

One of the most frequent mistakes in LDAP deployments is poor schema design or insufficient planning around directory structure. Many organizations rush into deployment without fully considering the long-term impact of how they organize objects, attributes, and hierarchical structures within the Directory Information Tree. A poorly designed schema can result in an overly complex or inconsistent structure that complicates directory management, hinders efficient searches, and creates challenges when delegating administrative control to different teams. Without clear planning, organizations may end up with redundant organizational units, improper use of object classes, or attributes that are not aligned with business requirements.

Another common pitfall is failing to properly configure access control lists. LDAP directories contain sensitive identity information, and without adequate ACLs, unauthorized users or applications may gain access to confidential data or perform unintended modifications. A lack of fine-grained access controls often results from default configurations being left unchanged or from blanket permissions being applied too broadly. This can expose user credentials, internal organizational structures, or other private information to anyone with basic directory access. Neglecting to define restrictive and well-scoped ACLs violates the principle of least privilege and creates serious security risks.

Neglecting encryption for LDAP traffic is another mistake that continues to affect organizations. Some deployments rely on unencrypted LDAP (port 389) for communication between clients and servers, leaving data such as usernames, passwords, and attribute values exposed to network sniffing or man-in-the-middle attacks.

While modern best practices recommend using LDAPS (port 636) or StartTLS to secure LDAP communications, many deployments still fail to implement transport layer encryption due to a lack of awareness or perceived configuration complexity. Failing to secure LDAP traffic undermines the confidentiality and integrity of identity-related data flowing through the network.

Improper replication design is a pitfall that affects both performance and availability. Many organizations implement LDAP replication to improve fault tolerance and distribute directory services geographically, but mistakes in replication topologies can lead to data inconsistencies, replication loops, or server overloads. For example, configuring multi-master replication without clear conflict resolution strategies can result in data divergence if conflicting updates occur simultaneously on different replicas. Similarly, overloading a single replica with excessive read or write operations due to poor load balancing can degrade performance and increase latency for end users.

Ignoring capacity planning and performance tuning is another recurring issue in LDAP deployments. As directory data grows and user populations expand, LDAP servers must be optimized to handle increased query loads and authentication requests. Failing to index frequently queried attributes can lead to slow search operations, while under-provisioned hardware can result in bottlenecks during peak usage periods. Additionally, excessive or unnecessary attribute indexing can consume more system resources than required, negatively affecting write performance. Organizations that overlook performance optimization early in the deployment often struggle to scale LDAP services effectively as business needs evolve.

Mismanaging password policies within LDAP is another area where deployments frequently fall short. Weak or inconsistent password policies can expose the organization to brute-force attacks, credential stuffing, or unauthorized account access. Some deployments rely on basic password complexity rules or fail to enforce policies such as password expiration, history, or lockout thresholds. Without robust password policies and regular policy reviews, organizations increase the risk of credential-based attacks on critical systems.

A common yet overlooked pitfall is the lack of proper monitoring and logging. LDAP servers generate logs that capture authentication events, directory modifications, and administrative actions, all of which are vital for security auditing and troubleshooting. However, many organizations fail to centralize and analyze these logs effectively, leaving them blind to unauthorized access attempts, replication failures, or configuration errors. Without real-time monitoring and alerting, LDAP administrators may not become aware of critical issues until they impact business operations or security postures.

Poor integration with enterprise applications is another challenge in LDAP environments. Some organizations deploy LDAP directories without fully understanding how existing applications interact with directory services. This often leads to broken authentication mechanisms, incomplete attribute mappings, or inconsistencies in how group memberships are interpreted by applications. Lack of testing during integration efforts can result in users being unable to authenticate to critical services, or worse, in applications not enforcing expected access controls based on directory data.

Underestimating the complexity of migration from legacy directory systems is another pitfall. Migrating from older directory services to modern LDAP implementations requires detailed planning around data transformation, schema mapping, and synchronization of identity information across platforms. Rushed or incomplete migrations can result in data loss, attribute mismatches, or disruption to dependent applications. Furthermore, without a rollback plan or parallel testing environment, organizations expose themselves to unnecessary operational risk.

Organizations also frequently neglect to account for directory service governance and documentation. LDAP environments that lack clear governance policies can quickly become disorganized, with inconsistent naming conventions, undocumented schema extensions, and ad hoc configuration changes. Without proper documentation, future administrators may face difficulties understanding the original design decisions, making it challenging to maintain, troubleshoot, or extend the directory over time.

Finally, one of the most pervasive pitfalls is treating LDAP deployment as a one-time project rather than an ongoing operational responsibility. Directory services require continuous attention to security patching, performance tuning, schema management, and integration updates. As new applications are onboarded and organizational structures evolve, LDAP environments must be maintained and adjusted accordingly. Failing to assign dedicated ownership or governance to directory services often leads to outdated configurations, security vulnerabilities, and poor user experiences.

Avoiding these common pitfalls requires a proactive and methodical approach to LDAP deployment. By investing time in planning, implementing robust security controls, optimizing for performance, and establishing clear governance practices, organizations can build resilient and scalable directory services that effectively support their identity and access management strategies. Recognizing and addressing these common mistakes early in the deployment process reduces operational risk and ensures that LDAP continues to deliver value as a core infrastructure component.

Final Thoughts and Best Practices

LDAP has firmly established itself as one of the foundational protocols for identity and directory services across enterprises of all sizes. Its ability to provide a structured, hierarchical, and highly extensible system for storing and managing identity data has ensured its relevance even as the IT landscape has evolved with the adoption of cloud, DevOps, and hybrid environments. As organizations continue to face new demands for security, scalability, and integration, LDAP's versatility continues to make it a key player in identity and access management strategies.

When deploying and managing LDAP directories, one of the most critical best practices is to prioritize a well-thought-out directory design. The structure of the Directory Information Tree must be intuitive, logical, and scalable to accommodate future growth. Organizations should avoid overly complex or flat structures and instead model the DIT to reflect their actual organizational hierarchy or business units. A clear and consistent naming convention should be established early on, promoting ease of use, delegating administration effectively, and reducing confusion as the directory grows.

Security should be baked into every stage of the LDAP deployment. Ensuring that all LDAP traffic is encrypted using TLS is a fundamental requirement to protect sensitive information during transmission. Strong authentication mechanisms, including secure bind methods and the integration of multi-factor authentication, further enhance directory security. Administrators must also implement granular access control lists that limit access to only those who require it, applying the principle of least privilege throughout the directory. Every attribute, object class, and organizational unit should be reviewed to determine the minimum necessary access permissions.

Performance tuning is another key best practice when operating LDAP at scale. Indexing plays a crucial role in the performance of search operations. Attributes that are frequently queried should be indexed to reduce search times and lower the load on LDAP servers. However, administrators must balance indexing carefully, as over-indexing can negatively impact write operations and resource consumption. Regularly reviewing usage patterns and query logs helps identify which attributes benefit most from indexing.

High availability and disaster recovery are essential considerations. LDAP directories often underpin critical services such as authentication for applications, VPNs, and network devices. Deploying redundant LDAP servers across multiple geographic locations and configuring proper replication ensures that the directory remains available even if individual servers or data centers experience downtime. Load balancing across LDAP servers can improve performance and resilience, distributing client requests to the most responsive server and preventing overloads on any single node. Additionally, implementing routine backup and recovery procedures protects against data corruption or accidental deletions, ensuring business continuity in the event of failures.

A proactive monitoring and alerting system should be in place to maintain directory health. Integrating LDAP server logs with centralized log management or SIEM solutions enables real-time visibility into authentication events, directory changes, and potential anomalies. Administrators can detect trends such as repeated failed login attempts, replication issues, or unauthorized access attempts. Regular health checks and monitoring of replication status, query response times, and system resource usage help identify and remediate performance bottlenecks before they affect users.

Another best practice is to approach LDAP schema extensions with caution. Extending the schema to add custom object classes or attributes is sometimes necessary to meet specific business requirements. However, these extensions should be thoroughly documented, reviewed, and aligned with established schema standards wherever possible. Excessive or poorly planned schema modifications can complicate application integrations and increase the likelihood of inconsistencies across environments. When custom attributes are introduced, they should follow naming conventions that prevent conflicts with existing or future schema elements.

Integration with external systems is a crucial part of maximizing LDAP's value. Many modern applications, cloud platforms, and identity providers can integrate with LDAP to centralize authentication and user management. When integrating LDAP with these systems, organizations should thoroughly test how user attributes, groups, and roles are mapped and utilized. Misaligned attribute mappings or group structures can result in improper access controls or failed authentication attempts. Continuous validation and documentation of these integrations are vital to maintaining secure and seamless workflows.

Automation is increasingly important for maintaining directory hygiene and operational efficiency. Scripts and configuration management tools should be employed to automate tasks such as account provisioning and deprovisioning, group membership management, and bulk directory updates. Automating these processes reduces manual intervention, minimizes errors, and ensures consistency across the environment. Leveraging Infrastructure as Code principles to manage LDAP configuration and deployment processes further enhances reliability and repeatability.

User education and governance should not be overlooked. Directory administrators, IT staff, and business stakeholders must be aligned on LDAP management policies, change control procedures, and security practices. Regular training sessions, coupled with detailed operational documentation, ensure that directory management remains consistent and compliant with internal policies and external regulations. Governance bodies or committees may be established to oversee LDAP-related changes and to review access control policies and schema updates periodically.

Compliance and audit readiness are also key considerations. Given that directories store sensitive identity information and play a central role in enforcing access controls, LDAP systems are often subject to regulatory scrutiny. Implementing proper logging, access reviews, and reporting tools helps organizations demonstrate compliance with regulations such as GDPR, HIPAA, and SOX. Scheduled audits of directory configurations, user accounts, and access permissions support continuous improvement and reduce the risk of non-compliance.

Finally, adopting a continuous improvement mindset ensures the long-term success of LDAP deployments. As new applications, cloud services, and business requirements emerge, the directory's design, security posture, and integrations should be revisited and updated as necessary. Regular reviews of directory usage patterns, security trends, and operational challenges allow organizations to adapt and modernize their LDAP environments in line with technological advancements and industry best practices.

LDAP's longevity and success in diverse IT environments are the result of its adaptability and robust design. When deployed thoughtfully and managed according to proven best practices, LDAP provides a secure, scalable, and reliable foundation for identity and access management that continues to meet the evolving needs of modern organizations. By emphasizing proper planning, security, performance optimization, and governance, organizations can ensure that LDAP remains a critical enabler of operational efficiency and security well into the future.

www.ingramcontent.com/pod-product-compliance
Lightning Source LLC
LaVergne TN
LVHW051233050326
832903LV00028B/2382